# SKINNY CHICKEN

# SKINNY CHICKEN

**ERICA LEVY KLEIN**

**Surrey Books**

Chicago

SKINNY CHICKEN is published by Surrey Books, Inc.
230 E. Ohio St., Suite 120, Chicago, IL 60611.

First edition: 1 2 3 4 5

This book is manufactured in the United States of America.

Library of Congress Cataloging-in-Publication data:

Klein, Erica Levy.
    Skinny chicken / by Erica Levy Klein.
    170p.  cm.
    Includes bibliographical references and index.
    ISBN 0-940625-88-1(cloth): $20.95 ISBN 0-940625-84-9 (pbk.): $12.95
    1. Low-fat diet—Recipes.  2. Cookery (Chicken).  I. Title.
RM237.7.K58 1994
641.5'638—dc20                                 94-8528
                                             CIP

Editorial and production: *Bookcrafters, Inc., Chicago*
Art Director: *Hughes & Co., Chicago*
Cover and interior illustrations by *Laurel DiGangi*
Back cover photos courtesy *California Olive Industry*

For free catalog and prices on quantity purchases, contact Surrey Books at the
address above.

This title is distributed to the trade by Publishers Group West.

**Other titles in the "Skinny" Cookbooks Series:**

| | |
|---|---|
| *Skinny Beef* | *Skinny Potatoes* |
| *Skinny Chocolate* | *Skinny Sauces & Marinades* |
| *Skinny Cookies, Cakes & Sweets* | *Skinny Seafood* |
| *Skinny One-Pot Meals* | *Skinny Soups* |
| *Skinny Pasta* | *Skinny Spices* |
| *Skinny Pizzas* | |

**For Mildred Levy**
who would have laughed at the idea
of a skinny chicken

# CONTENTS

# FOREWORD

**T**here was a time in the days of my European Jewish ancestors when having a chicken for Sabbath dinner meant you were either very wealthy or very lucky. Today, chicken is considered more or less an everyday occurrence; an inexpensive source of protein that is usually "on special" at every other supermarket across the country.

It's really not surprising that chicken has gone from a rare commodity to an overexposed bird. The supply of chickens continues to be plentiful, and what's more, chickens are always engaging in behavior guaranteed to result in even more chickens. If overpopulation wasn't bad enough for chicken PR, virtually every diet program in the country puts chicken on the short list with low-fat cottage cheese and fish. So it's no wonder that Americans take chicken completely for granted!

That's why I'm so pleased that the publisher of Surrey Books asked me to develop this all-new collection of delicious, healthy chicken recipes. These low-fat, low-sodium recipes are organized into three main sections: The Casual Chicken, featuring familiar favorites and chicken classics; The Quick Chicken, for meals on the run; and The Dressy Chicken, a healthy resource for fancier fare. In my opinion, chicken has deserved an entirely new image for a long time!

There is also a rather personal reason why I chose to write this cookbook. According to my mother, who passed away in 1988, the only meat I would eat as a child was skinless chicken, and to this day, I can think of no clearer sensory memory than the smell of her slowly roasting chicken wafting through the house on all those Friday nights.

In writing *Skinny Chicken*, I benefited from the capable assistance of nutritional research consultant Leslie Weinstein, who I'm convinced has chicken soup in her blood. And from the loyalty and support of my husband, Ken Kroll, the ultimate taste tester, who sometimes gave me suggestions for adding more spices or cutting back on salt at one or two in the morning.

I would also like to acknowledge the generosity of the Food Safety and Inspection Service of the American Department of Agriculture and the Communications Division of the National Broiler Council for allowing me to use material from several of their highly informative brochures.

I will close with this simple culinary prayer: May you always find two chickens in every pot, and cook them using recipes from this book to make each one taste better than the other. And may your only challenge be deciding which chicken dish you enjoy more.

Erica Levy Klein

# COOKING BY
# THE NUMBERS
*A Note about the Nutritional Data*

**A**lthough nutritional information is provided for each recipe in this book, you should remember that nutritional data is rarely—if ever—infallible. The recipe analysis figures were derived using software highly regarded by nutritionists and dietitians. The figures are based on actual lab values of ingredients rather than general rules of thumb, such as each fat gram contains 9 calories, and therefore may vary from the results of traditional formulas used to calculate total calories from fat.

To keep fat at a minimum in any chicken recipe, it is best to choose white meat instead of dark, remove the skin either before or after cooking, and use the lowest-fat cooking methods such as grilling or broiling.

Other factors affecting nutritional data include: the variable sizes of vegetables and fruits; a plus or minus 20 percent error factor on the nutritional labels of packaged foods; and cooking techniques and appliances.

Please also note that when you see the phrase "salt and pepper to taste," it means these ingredients are optional and are not figured into the nutritional analysis. And when there are two choices for ingredients, such as "chicken, *or* fish stock," the *first* listed item is the one used to develop the nutritional data. Ingredients listed as "optional" are not included in the data.

If you have any health problem that mandates strict dietary requirements, it is important that you consult a physician, clinical dietitian, or nutritionist before proceeding with any recipe in this book. Also, if you are a diabetic or require a diet that restricts calories, fat, or sodium, remember that the nutritional analysis figures may be accurate for the recipe we tested but not for the food you cooked due to the variables.

Use these low-fat, low-calorie recipes as a starting point for healthier eating, but regard all of the nutritional figures only as general guidelines for planning delicious and memorable meals.

# 1.
# CHICKEN 101:
# A POULTRY PRIMER

### *Meet the Low-Fat, High-Taste Champ*

I t's not coincidental that at the same time America is changing the way it eats, consumption of chicken is on the rise.

The nation has slowly but surely become more fitness conscious and more discriminating in its daily diet. And today, contemporary living calls for lighter, healthier, well-balanced meals that are lower in fat, calories, cholesterol, sugar, and salt.

It's no wonder then, that chicken, with lower fat than most red meats, has increasingly become a popular source of animal protein.

Busier, active lifestyles require not only lighter and leaner cuisine but also convenience and taste appeal. So gone are yesterday's on-and-off fad diets and harsh weight-loss programs. In their place are consistent, balanced programs, combining nutrition and exercise, aimed at maintaining lifelong health and well-being.

Chicken, of course, fits right in. Chicken appeals equally to children, teenagers, and adults. Chicken is also a highly convenient food, adapting readily to the fast preparation times and flexible eating schedules that families and singles often require. And to top it off, chicken makes about as economical a meal as you can find anywhere.

# 2.
# GETTING THE SKINNY ON CHICKEN

**N**ot surprisingly, excess fat in the nation's diet continues to be *the* major issue in nutrition today. Health organizations such as the American Heart Association recommend that no more than 30 percent of total daily calories come from fat and less than one-third of the "fat calories" from saturated fat.

Saturated fat is a true villain—a major contributor to elevated blood cholesterol. Unsaturated fat, on the other hand, can actually help to lower blood cholesterol. And that's just one of the many reasons why chicken makes a smart meal choice. The total fat content of a 3-ounce skinless portion of whole roasted chicken is less than *half* that of beef and about *one-third* that of pork. And most of the fat chicken does contain is unsaturated—the good-guys-in-the-white-hats kind of cholesterol-lowering fat.

The chart below illustrates exactly how chicken stacks up nutritionally:

## *Nutrition Breakdown per Serving*

**Percent of recommended daily dietary intake***

| | Qty. | | 0% | 50% | 100% |
|---|---|---|---|---|---|
| Calories | 134 | 7 | | | |
| Total Fat | 4.1 g | 6 | | | |
| Cholesterol | 76 mg | 24 | | | |
| Sodium | 73 mg | 2 | | | |
| Protein | 23 g | 51 | | | |
| Iron | 1 mg | 6 | | | |

Figures are for a 3-oz. serving of roasted, skinless whole chicken. A 3-oz. serving of cooked chicken breast is even more nutritionally beneficial: 116 calories and 1.5g total fat.

*Recommended daily intake is based on: calories, 2,000; fat, no more than 30% of calories; cholesterol, 300 mg; sodium 3,300 mg.

Courtesy: National Broiler Council

## *Amazing Chickeny Facts*

♦ *Fact #1*   Did you know that baked or broiled chicken meat has the same fat and calorie content regardless of whether or not the skin is removed prior to cooking? Unlike beef fat, the fat in chicken skin stays put and doesn't travel into the muscles. Leaving skin on during cooking helps seal in moisture and may even eliminate the need for an oil-based marinade. Removing the skin after cooking cuts the already low fat content almost in half.

♦ *Fact #2*   Chicken is a good choice for low-sodium diets. The National Academy of Sciences recommends an upper limit of 3300 milligrams of sodium daily, although many nutritionists advocate a limit that is even lower. A 3-ounce serving of skinless chicken contains just 73 milligrams of sodium—a taste bargain if there ever was one!

♦ *Fact #3*   All calories are not equal. One gram of protein contains four calories. One gram of fat contains nine calories. Not only that, the body metabolizes excess protein calories more easily while fat calories convert more readily to body fat. That's what makes low-fat chicken such a smart protein source.

♦ ***Fact #4*** Many traditionally higher-fat recipes can be adapted to healthier standards by replacing calorie-laden ingredients with chicken. Try using ground chicken instead of ground red meats in your favorite chili, meatloaf, spaghetti sauce, or hamburger recipes.

♦ ***Fact #5*** For a 2,000-calorie-per-day diet, a 3-ounce serving of chicken breast (one breast-half), baked or roasted and served without skin, contains only 2 percent of the recommended maximum daily fat intake, only 1.8 percent of the recommended maximum saturated fat intake, and only 24 percent of the recommended maximum cholesterol intake.

# 3.

# CHICKEN *PART*-ICULARS

**Y**es, there really is such a group called the National Broiler Council, which I suppose is preferable to calling themselves the National Chicken Cluckers Council, although the latter may technically be more accurate. This group is the trade association for the hardworking farmers across the country who raise broiler chickens. I understand the lobbyists for the National Broiler Council are so underpaid that they often work for chicken feed. (Sorry, but could you have resisted an opportunity like that?)

At any rate, the National Broiler Council offers the following step-by-step techniques that can simplify the process of cutting up a whole chicken or of deboning selected chicken parts:

## *Cutting Up a Whole Chicken*

Chicken is usually one of the best buys at the supermarket in any given week. You'll save even more when you purchase whole birds and cut them up yourself.

♦ **1.** Place chicken, breast side up, on cutting board. Cut skin between thighs and body.

♦ **2.** Grasping one leg in each hand, lift chicken and bend back legs until bones break at hip joints.

♦ **3.** Remove leg-thigh from body by cutting (from tail toward shoulder) between the joints, close to bones in back of bird. Repeat on other side.

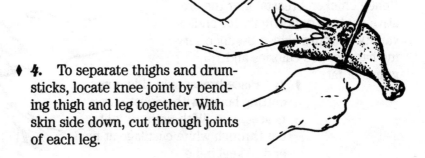

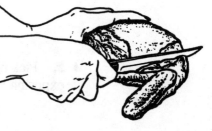

♦ **4.** To separate thighs and drumsticks, locate knee joint by bending thigh and leg together. With skin side down, cut through joints of each leg.

♦ **5.** With chicken on back, remove wings by cutting inside of wing just over joint. Pull wing away from body and cut from top down, through joint.

♦ **6.** Separate breast and back by placing chicken on neck-end or back and cutting (toward board) through joints along each side of rib cage.

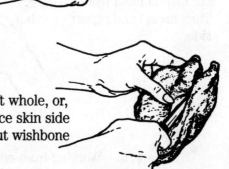

♦ **7.** Breast may be left whole, or, to cut into halves, place skin side down on board and cut wishbone in two at V of bone.

# Boning a Whole Chicken Breast

Boned chicken breasts offer the creative cook an opportunity for endless variety. Without skin, a 3-ounce serving has just 116 calories and 1.5 grams of fat.

♦ **1.** Place breast skin side down on cutting board with widest part nearest you. With point of knife, cut through white cartilage at neck end of keel bone.

♦ **2.** Pick up breast and bend back, exposing keel bone.

♦ **3.** Loosen meat from bone by running thumbs around both sides; pull out bone and cartilage.

♦ **4.** Working one side of breast, insert tip of knife under long rib bone inside thin membrane and cut or pull meat from rib cage. Turn breast and repeat on other side.

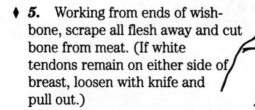

♦ **5.** Working from ends of wishbone, scrape all flesh away and cut bone from meat. (If white tendons remain on either side of breast, loosen with knife and pull out.)

## *Boning Half a Chicken Breast*

Packages of chicken breast at the supermarket often contain four half-breasts, the usual serving for four.

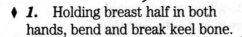

♦ *1.*  Holding breast half in both hands, bend and break keel bone.

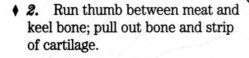

♦ *2.*  Run thumb between meat and keel bone; pull out bone and strip of cartilage.

♦ *3.*  Using both thumbs, loosen meat from rib cage.

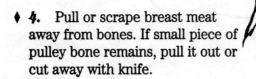

♦ *4.*  Pull or scrape breast meat away from bones. If small piece of pulley bone remains, pull it out or cut away with knife.

## *Boning a Chicken Thigh*

For those who prefer dark meat,
boned chicken thighs can be used in
many imaginative chicken dishes.

♦ **1.** Place thigh on cutting board,
skin side down, and cut along thin
side, joint to joint.

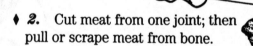

♦ **2.** Cut meat from one joint; then
pull or scrape meat from bone.

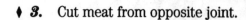

♦ **3.** Cut meat from opposite joint.

# 4.
# HEALTHY CONCERNS: CARE AND HANDLING

**A** ccording to the U.S. Department of Agriculture, seven million people get sick from food poisoning each year, many of them from improperly handled or stored chicken. The good news is that there are easy ways to prevent yourself from becoming a statistic.

The USDA recommends the following tips for keeping food-borne organisms from making themselves at home:

♦ Freeze fresh chicken immediately if you can't use it within a few days. Thaw in refrigerator, not on the counter.

♦ Put packages of frozen poultry on a plate before thawing in refrigerator so their juices won't drip on other foods as they defrost.

♦ Cook poultry to 160 degrees or until all juices run clear.

♦ If you're microwaving chicken, be aware that the microwaving process can leave cold spots where bacteria breed. Observe the standing time called for in a recipe because this is when microwaved food finishes cooking.

♦ When you cook ahead in large quantities, divide batches into small, shallow containers for refrigeration. This ensures safe, rapid cooling.

♦ Serve grilled chicken on a clean plate, *not* the one that held the raw poultry.

♦ Never leave perishable food out of the refrigerator for more than 2 hours.

♦ If you pack cooked chicken for a picnic, carry it in a cooler with a cold pack. When possible, put the cooler in the shade. Keep the lid on as much as you can.

♦ At a party, keep cold cooked chicken or chicken salad on ice, or serve it in batches throughout the gathering from platters stored in the refrigerator.

♦ If you're serving stuffed chicken or turkey, remove the stuffing and refrigerate poultry and stuffing in separate containers.

♦ Finally, this is the *maximum* length of time you should keep fresh or cooked chicken refrigerated or frozen before discarding:

|  | **Refrigerator** (40° F) | **Freezer** (0° F) |
| --- | --- | --- |
| Fresh whole chicken | 1-2 days | 1 year |
| Fresh chicken pieces | 1-2 days | 9 months |
| Fresh chicken giblets | 1-2 days | 3-4 months |
| Cooked fried chicken | 3-4 days | 4 months |
| Cooked chicken dishes | 3-4 days | 4-6 months |
| Cooked chicken pieces | 3-4 days | 4 months |
| Cooked chicken pieces covered with broth/sauce | 1-2 days | 6 months |
| Cooked chicken patties | 1-2 days | 1-3 months |

# 5.

# 7 Delicious Cooking Techniques Chickens Adore

**M**onotony is the enemy of good nutrition and dulls the appetite (not to mention people!). Chicken is such a versatile food, it could be eaten every day in the year and prepared differently every time.

The best strategy is to use cooking methods that don't rob chicken of its natural nutritional value—or add extra calories. Some preferred methods are:

♦ ***Roasted or Baked*** Place whole bird in 375-degree oven for 1 hour or until juices run clear when pierced with a fork. Bake light meat parts in 350-degree oven for 35-40 minutes; bake dark meat parts about 45 minutes.

♦ ***Oven Fried*** Using bone-in parts, dip chicken first in beaten egg white, then in seasoned breadcrumbs. Place on lightly greased baking sheet, and bake in 375-degree oven for about 40 minutes or until brown and fork can be inserted in chicken with ease.

♦ *Grilled or Broiled*   Place chicken, skin side up, on prepared grill with rack 6-8 inches over ashen coals. Turn frequently during cooking. Any parts may be used, and chicken may be marinated or basted. Use the same procedure for broiling.

♦ *Microwaved*   Follow manufacturer's instructions, but in general, allow 6 minutes per pound on High (100%), except for a whole bird, which cooks best on Medium (50%). Cover with wax paper; season after cooking but before standing time.

♦ *Sautéed*   Boneless breast halves, fillets, cutlets, diced meat, or patties are time-savers when sautéed in small amount of chicken broth over medium-high heat; about 2-3 minutes per side.

♦ *Stir-Fried*   Use any chicken part cut into strips. Place chicken in small amount of polyunsaturated oil over high heat. Cook, stirring frequently, about 5 minutes or until no longer pink.

♦ *Poached or Simmered*   Place chicken, whole or in parts, in saucepan with enough water to cover. Simmer about 45 minutes or until fork can be inserted in chicken with ease.

# 6.
# HERBS AND SPICES THAT LOVE CHICKEN

**I**f the mere thought of chicken is starting to make you think seriously about being a vegetarian, it's time to liven things up with one of the following herbs or spices—all of which can turn an ordinary chicken into an extraordinary meal.

In case you've always wondered if there was a difference between herbs and spices (the two terms are often used interchangably) there really is. Herbs are the soft leafy part of the plant; spices are the hard portion of the plant including the seeds, root, bark, or berries.

♦ **allspice** its scent is reminiscent of cinnamon, cloves, and nutmeg "all" rolled into one. Very powerful, so use sparingly. Especially good in curry sauces.

◆ **anise**   a sweet, licorice-like taste that's terrific when used in moderation. Toast the seeds first in a little canola oil.

◆ **basil**   sweet and pungent; great in garlicky, tomato-based sauces or in Thai sauces. Good in marinades too.

◆ **bay leaf**   a strong taste that adds depth and texture to chicken stews or chicken chili.

◆ **caraway**   has a mild, tangy quality that's similar to dill seed.

◆ **cardamon** (also spelled **cardamom**)   sharp, pungent and sweet with a cinnamon-like aroma. Use just a little to balance out the ingredients of a chicken curry.

◆ **cayenne pepper**   the tongue-searing red pepper that adds a kick to Creole, Cajun, and Tex-Mex sauces.

◆ **celery seed**   celery-like flavor that zips up chicken salad and marinades.

◆ **chervil leaf**   a strong, herbal taste with just a hint of tarragon.

◆ **chives**   a mild onion taste that can be incorporated into sauces or used as a colorful garnish.

◆ **cilantro**   also known as Chinese parsley and coriander leaf. Better and more flavorful in its fresh form, although some people may suffer an allergic reaction. A natural addition to Asian or Mexican chicken soups.

◆ **cinnamon**   sweet, fragrant, and versatile enough to spice up everything from curry sauces to dessert sauces.

◆ **cloves**   a type of evergreen bud typically found in pungent marinades or sweet sauces. A key ingredient in Chinese five-spice chicken dishes.

◆ **coriander**   cilantro in its seed form, spicy and citrus-like. Good in chili or to flavor chicken stock.

◆ **cumin**   the major flavor ingredient in most chili powders. Good in Indian or Latin American dishes. Blends especially well with yogurt.

◆ **dill weed**   the feathery leaf of the dill plant, with a pungent kick and light, heady fragrance. Wonderful in lemon-based chicken recipes.

◆ **fennel seed**   a licorice taste similar to anise but much milder. Use sparingly so as not to overpower the tender flavor of chicken.

◆ **fenugreek**   spicy, slightly bitter maple-like flavor typically found in the more authentic curry sauces.

◆ **garlic**   an ideal addition to any chicken dish. New varieties like Dr. Sakai's Garlic will even leave your breath smelling sweet! Use sparingly to add dimension; add more to increase garlicky kick.

◆ **ginger**   a sharp, spicy-sweet flavor that wakes up Asian and Indian chicken dishes.

♦ **horseradish**   a white root powder with a hot, hearty flavor. The pow-der is even more intense than the prepared bottled variety, so exercise caution.

♦ **mace**   the ground outer covering of nutmeg, with a more compelling, pungent fragrance.

♦ **marjoram**   a milder cousin of oregano. Good in Mediterranean chicken recipes.

♦ **mint**   light, fragrant, and tangy at the same time. A good counterpoint to garlic, or use it to add a pleasing contrast in Thai chicken dishes.

♦ **mustard powder**   hot and spicy; a tangy addition to vinaigrette style chicken marinades.

♦ **nutmeg**   mild, nutty, and fragrant.

♦ **oregano**   the dominant herb in most Italian sauces. Try it in a ground chicken spaghetti sauce.

♦ **paprika**   a mild, ground reddish pepper that's the main seasoning in chicken paprikash.

♦ **parsley**   the ever-present garnish, with a mild herbal flavor that some-times is hard to distinguish from other ingredients.

♦ **pepper**   a spicy berry with many varieties, including black, green, pink and white.

♦ **poppy seed**   tiny seeds with a sweetish, nutty taste and texture. Combined with chicken in the Middle East.

♦ **rosemary**   fragrant, strongly flavored leaf that looks like a miniature pine needle. Remove before serving to avoid puncturing the mouth or tongue.

♦ **saffron**   the most expensive of all spices because of the number of flowers needed to obtain just a small amount. A traditional accompani-ment for many Indian, Spanish, and Mediterranean chicken dishes.

♦ **sage**   strong, pleasant flavor with a sweet, herbal fragrance.

♦ **savory**   a mild, thyme-like taste that adds special fragrance to chicken.

♦ **sesame seed**   mild, nut-like flavor that improves with roasting in a lit-tle oil first. Use as a major ingredient or as a pleasing garnish.

♦ **tarragon leaf**   a rich, sweet flavor faintly reminiscent of anise. A won-derful complement to cold or hot chicken.

♦ **thyme**   distinctive, pleasant herbal flavor and fragrance that's wonder-ful in European-inspired chicken dishes.

♦ **turmeric**   a brilliant yellow ground spice with a peppery aroma and ginger-like flavor. Adds the golden color to curry powder.

# 7.

# THE CASUAL CHICKEN
### *Tasty Favorites*

♦

# EASY, CHEESY CHICKEN CORN CHOWDER

**Serves 4**

½ cup onion, finely chopped
½ cup water
1 cup cooked, boneless chicken, skin removed,
  meat cubed
1 large (17-oz.) can and 1 small (8½-oz.) can
  creamed corn
3 cups skim milk
  Salt, *or* salt substitute and pepper to taste
6 ozs. reduced-fat Cheddar cheese, grated

**A**dd water and onion to large saucepan, and cook over medium heat 5-6 minutes, until onion is tender. Drain off water. Add chicken, creamed corn, milk, salt or salt substitute, and pepper and bring to boil.

Reduce heat and gradually stir in small amounts of cheese until melted. Do *not* bring to boil again. Serve immediately.

### Nutritional Data

| PER SERVING | | EXCHANGES | |
|---|---|---|---|
| Calories: | 279 | Milk: | 0.9 |
| Fat (gm): | 6.3 | Vegetable: | 0.2 |
| Sat. fat (gm): | 2.9 | Fruit: | 0.0 |
| Cholesterol (mg): | 60.8 | Bread: | 1.4 |
| Sodium (mg): | 673 | Meat: | 3.0 |
| % Calories from fat: | 14 | Fat: | 0.0 |

# CHICK 'N PEA SOUP

**Serves 8**

2 cups cooked, boneless chicken, skin removed,
  meat cubed
8 cups defatted chicken stock
1 16-oz. package dried green split peas
2 carrots, peeled, cut into small cubes
1 cup onion, chopped
  Salt substitute and ground pepper to taste

 ombine all ingredients in large pot. Bring to boil, reduce heat,
and simmer 1 hour, stirring occasionally.

### Nutritional Data

| PER SERVING | | EXCHANGES | |
| --- | --- | --- | --- |
| Calories: | 241 | Milk: | 0.0 |
| Fat (gm): | 4.4 | Vegetable: | 0.5 |
| Sat. fat (gm): | 1.1 | Fruit: | 0.0 |
| Cholesterol (mg): | 48.2 | Bread: | 2.0 |
| Sodium (mg): | 792 | Meat: | 2.4 |
| % Calories from fat: | 11 | Fat: | 0.0 |

# LIGHT AND "CREAMY" POTATO-CHICKEN SOUP

### Serves 6

2 cups potatoes, peeled and diced

3/4 cup onion, chopped

1 1/2 cups cooked boneless chicken, skin removed, meat cubed

1 16-oz. can creamed corn

3 cups skim milk

Salt, *or* salt substitute, and ground pepper to taste

P lace potatoes and onion in large saucepan, cover with water, bring to low boil, and cook 15-20 minutes. Drain off water. Add remaining ingredients, and heat through but do *not* bring to boil.

### Nutritional Data

| PER SERVING | | EXCHANGES | |
|---|---|---|---|
| Calories: | 281 | Milk: | 0.5 |
| Fat (gm): | 5.1 | Vegetable: | 0.2 |
| Sat. fat (gm): | 1.5 | Fruit: | 0.0 |
| Cholesterol (mg): | 49.8 | Bread: | 1.4 |
| Sodium (mg): | 323 | Meat: | 2.0 |
| % Calories from fat: | 16 | Fat: | 0.0 |

# Hong Kong Jewish Chicken Soup

***Serves 7*** *(1 cup each)*

  2  lbs. chicken, skin removed

10  cups cold water

 ⅓  cup rice wine, *or* sake

  4  slices (about 1 tablespoon) fresh ginger

**B**lanch chicken in large pot of boiling water 1 minute; then drain and rinse pieces under cold water. Rinse out pot.

Add 10 cups of water, chicken, wine, and ginger. Bring to boil. Skim off froth and allow to simmer, uncovered, 1½ hours.

Remove chicken (freeze to use later in recipes calling for cooked chicken) and ginger. Allow soup to cool uncovered. Refrigerate and skim off any fat before serving.

---

### Nutritional Data

| PER SERVING | | EXCHANGES | |
|---|---|---|---|
| Calories: | 194 | Milk: | 0.0 |
| Fat (gm): | 6.9 | Vegetable: | 0.0 |
| Sat. fat (gm): | 1.4 | Fruit: | 0.1 |
| Cholesterol (mg): | 100 | Bread: | 0.0 |
| Sodium (mg): | 145 | Meat: | 4.6 |
| % Calories from fat: | 19 | Fat: | 0.3 |

# ITALIAN CHICKEN SOUP

### Serves 8

1 lb. lean chicken, ground
2 slices whole wheat bread, crumbled
3 tablespoons Parmesan cheese, grated
2 tablespoons fresh parsley, chopped
1 egg, lightly beaten
1 teaspoon garlic, minced
1 teaspoon lemon rind, grated
¼ teaspoon nutmeg, grated
Salt substitute and ground pepper to taste
10 cups defatted chicken stock

C ombine all ingredients, except chicken stock, and mix well. Form into small meatballs. In large saucepan, bring stock to full boil. Carefully drop in meatballs, cover, reduce heat, and simmer 6-8 minutes. Serve soup hot and garnish with additional fresh chopped parsley if desired.

### Nutritional Data

| PER SERVING | | EXCHANGES | |
|---|---|---|---|
| Calories: | 147 | Milk: | 0.0 |
| Fat (gm): | 4 | Vegetable: | 0.0 |
| Sat. fat (gm): | 1.4 | Fruit: | 0.0 |
| Cholesterol (mg): | 61.2 | Bread: | 0.2 |
| Sodium (mg): | 791 | Meat: | 1.7 |
| % Calories from fat: | 26 | Fat: | 0.1 |

# PARMESAN CHICKEN NIBBLES

### Serves 16

½ cup Dijon mustard
4 tablespoons low-sodium white wine
1 cup Italian breadcrumbs
½ cup Parmesan cheese, grated
2½ lbs. chicken pieces, skin removed
  Non-stick cooking spray

P reheat oven to 375 degrees. Combine mustard and white wine until it reaches consistency of dipping sauce. Set aside. Combine breadcrumbs and cheese.

Dip each chicken piece in mustard mixture and shake off excess. Roll each piece in breadcrumb mixture.

Place chicken on cookie sheet coated with non-stick spray, and bake 45 minutes. Serve hot or cold.

### Nutritional Data

| PER SERVING | | EXCHANGES | |
|---|---|---|---|
| Calories: | 185 | Milk: | 0.0 |
| Fat (gm): | 9.5 | Vegetable: | 0.1 |
| Sat. fat (gm): | 3.5 | Fruit: | 0.0 |
| Cholesterol (mg): | 50 | Bread: | 0.3 |
| Sodium (mg): | 299 | Meat: | 2.5 |
| % Calories from fat: | 13 | Fat: | 0.3 |

# Colleen's Oven-Fried Chicken Tenders

*Serves 9*

1   2-lb. chicken, meat cut into large strips
1   cup all-purpose flour
1½  teaspoons seasoning salt, *or* salt substitute
1   teaspoon ground black pepper
3   tablespoons canola oil
    Non-stick cooking spray

**P**reheat oven to 350 degrees. Shake chicken in plastic bag with flour, seasoning salt (or salt substitute), and pepper.

Heat oil in large skillet. Add chicken, and brown over medium heat on both sides. Remove chicken and place in large baking pan or casserole sprayed with non-stick spray. Cover and bake 45 minutes or until cooked through.

*Nutritional Data*

| PER SERVING | | EXCHANGES | |
|---|---|---|---|
| Calories: | 200 | Milk: | 0.0 |
| Fat (gm): | 16 | Vegetable: | 0.0 |
| Sat. fat (gm): | 4.8 | Fruit: | 0.0 |
| Cholesterol (mg): | 91.9 | Bread: | 0.8 |
| Sodium (mg): | 510 | Meat: | 4.1 |
| % Calories from fat: | 26 | Fat: | 1.1 |

# RANCH-STYLE BAKED CHICKEN TEASERS

*Serves 8*

½ cup whole wheat flour
2 eggs, lightly beaten
½ cup buttermilk
1 tablespoon Dijon mustard
1 cup wheat flakes, crushed, *or* corn flakes
1 teaspoon paprika
  Salt, *or* salt substitute, and ground pepper to taste
8 chicken thighs, cut in half, skin removed
  Non-stick cooking spray
1 tablespoon unsalted diet margarine

**P**reheat oven to 425 degrees. Spoon flour onto plate.
Whisk together eggs, buttermilk, and mustard in shallow bowl.
Mix together cereal flakes, paprika, salt (or salt substitute), and pepper
and spoon onto another plate.

Dip chicken pieces first in flour, then egg mixture, then cereal flakes
mixture. Place chicken in large baking pan coated with non-stick spray.
Dot with diet margarine, and bake 30 minutes.

### Nutritional Data

| PER SERVING | | EXCHANGES | |
|---|---|---|---|
| Calories: | 198 | Milk: | 0.1 |
| Fat (gm): | 17.1 | Vegetable: | 0.0 |
| Sat. fat (gm): | 5.2 | Fruit: | 0.1 |
| Cholesterol (mg): | 50 | Bread: | 0.3 |
| Sodium (mg): | 237 | Meat: | 2.9 |
| % Calories from fat: | 25 | Fat: | 2.7 |

# SPRING STEW WITH HERBED CHICKEN AND VEGETABLES

*Serves 4*

2 lb. fryer chicken, skin removed
2/3 lb. baking potatoes
1 medium onion, finely chopped
3 garlic cloves, minced
3 medium carrots, peeled, cut into 1-inch pieces
2 celery stalks, cut into 1-inch pieces
1/2 lb. mushrooms, cut in halves
1/2 tablespoon fresh sage
1 teaspoon fresh marjoram leaves
2 tablespoons fresh dill
2 sprigs fresh thyme
1/2 teaspoon salt
1/2 teaspoon ground black pepper

**I**n large uncovered saucepan, simmer chicken in 2 quarts water 1 hour. In separate covered saucepan, boil potatoes in 1 quart water 40 minutes; set aside.

Remove chicken from pot, reserving stock, and allow to cool until able to handle. Remove and discard skin. Remove all meat and set aside. Discard remaining bones and carcass. Skim all fat from top of stock and set aside.

In large saucepan, sauté onion and garlic 2 minutes over medium heat. Add carrots, celery, mushrooms, and 1 cup stock; simmer 10 minutes. Add chicken pieces, herbs, seasonings, and 1 more cup stock; cook an additional 10 minutes, uncovered.

Remove skins from potatoes, cut potatoes into chunks, and add to stew before serving.

### Nutritional Data

| PER SERVING | | EXCHANGES | |
|---|---|---|---|
| Calories: | 311 | Milk: | 0.0 |
| Fat (gm): | 3.3 | Vegetable: | 1.8 |
| Sat. fat (gm): | 1 | Fruit: | 0.0 |
| Cholesterol (mg): | 98 | Bread: | 0.8 |
| Sodium (mg): | 437 | Meat: | 7.? |
| % Calories from fat: | 9 | Fat: | 0.0 |

# PLOUGHMAN'S CHICKEN

### *Serves 6*

2 teaspoons olive oil
1 large onion, thinly sliced
2 stalks celery, cut into 1-inch pieces
3 lbs. chicken pieces, skin removed
½ cup vermouth
¾ cup defatted chicken stock
1 teaspoon garlic, minced
½ teaspoon dried thyme
Salt, *or* salt substitute and ground pepper to taste
4 new potatoes, cut into 1½-inch cubes
Parsley

**H**eat oil in large skillet and sauté onion and celery over medium heat 3-4 minutes. Add chicken, increase heat, and cook 1 minute. Add vermouth and bring to boil for 1 minute.

Add remaining ingredients, except potatoes and parsley, bring to boil, and lower to simmer for 10 minutes. Add potatoes and simmer, covered, another 30-35 minutes. Garnish with parsley and serve.

### *Nutritional Data*

| PER SERVING | | EXCHANGES | |
|---|---|---|---|
| Calories: | 215 | Milk: | 0.0 |
| Fat (gm): | 24.2 | Vegetable: | 0.3 |
| Sat. fat (gm): | 6.3 | Fruit: | 0.1 |
| Cholesterol (mg): | 100 | Bread: | 0.7 |
| Sodium (mg): | 277 | Meat: | 7.3 |
| % Calories from fat: | 29 | Fat: | 0.7 |

# CHICKEN CHINA MOON

***Serves 4***

1 tablespoon sesame seeds, toasted
2 teaspoons ginger, grated
Sweetener equivalent to 2 tablespoons sugar
2 tablespoons low-sodium soy sauce
Non-stick cooking spray
4 boneless chicken breast halves, skin removed,
pounded thin
2 tablespoons chopped green onion

C ombine sesame seeds, ginger, sweetener, and soy sauce and stir well. Apply non-stick spray to grill or broiling pan. Using sesame-soy mixture for basting, grill chicken over medium hot coals—or broil— 4 minutes on each side until cooked through. Garnish with green onion and serve.

### Nutritional Data

| PER SERVING | | EXCHANGES | |
|---|---|---|---|
| Calories: | 268 | Milk: | 0.0 |
| Fat (gm): | 14.5 | Vegetable: | 0.0 |
| Sat. fat (gm): | 4.0 | Fruit: | 0.0 |
| Cholesterol (mg): | 92.8 | Bread: | 0.0 |
| Sodium (mg): | 406 | Meat: | 4.0 |
| % Calories from fat: | 28 | Fat: | 0.3 |

# CANTONESE CHICKEN

***Serves 6***

2 lbs. chicken pieces, skin removed
6 dried Chinese or Japanese shiitake mushrooms
  soaked in hot water 20-30 minutes, squeezed
  dry, cut into strips
3 tablespoons low-sodium soy sauce
2 tablespoons oyster sauce
2 tablespoons dry cooking sherry
2 teaspoons garlic, minced
2 teaspoons fresh ginger, minced
1½ tablespoons arrowroot
1 teaspoon sesame oil
  Sweetener equivalent to ½ teaspoon sugar
  Salt, *or* salt substitute, to taste
2 tablespoons peanut oil
4 scallions, green parts only, cut into 2-inch
  lengths

**P**lace chicken and mushrooms in large mixing bowl. In separate dish, combine all remaining ingredients except peanut oil and scallions. Pour sauce mixture over chicken and mushrooms, toss well, cover, and marinate at room temperature 30-40 minutes.

In large covered baking pan, heat peanut oil over high heat, and stir-fry scallions 1 minute. Add chicken and marinade. Stir-fry 2 minutes to brown on all sides. Cover, reduce heat, and cook 30 minutes, stirring occasionally.

***Nutritional Data***

| PER SERVING | | EXCHANGES | |
|---|---|---|---|
| Calories: | 204 | Milk: | 0.0 |
| Fat (gm): | 11.4 | Vegetable: | 1.8 |
| Sat. fat (gm): | 3.1 | Fruit: | 0.0 |
| Cholesterol (mg): | 100 | Bread: | 0.1 |
| Sodium (mg): | 768 | Meat: | 5.5 |
| % Calories from fat: | 27 | Fat: | 1.0 |

# VERMONT TRIED-AND-TRUE BARBECUE

---

### Serves 4

⅛ cup white wine vinegar
1 teaspoon salt
1 tablespoon canola oil
1 chicken, cut up, skin removed
**Vermont Barbecue Sauce** (see recipe below)

**C**ombine vinegar and salt and whisk in oil. Place chicken pieces in large bowl or dish, and pour marinade over all. Cover and chill overnight.

Grill chicken on oiled rack 10-12 minutes per side. Baste with Vermont Barbecue Sauce, and grill another 2 minutes. Serve with remaining sauce.

### Vermont Barbecue Sauce

1 small onion, finely chopped
1½ teaspoons canola oil
1½ teaspoons Worcestershire sauce
¾ teaspoon Dijon mustard
¼ cup ketchup
½ cup defatted chicken stock

Sauté onion in oil in small saucepan until soft, about 3 minutes. Stir in remaining ingredients and bring to boil. Simmer 4-5 minutes. Allow to cool, and use as basting sauce.

---

### Nutritional Data

| PER SERVING | | EXCHANGES | |
|---|---|---|---|
| Calories: | 198 | Milk: | 0.0 |
| Fat (gm): | 6.8 | Vegetable: | 0.2 |
| Sat. fat (gm): | 1.1 | Fruit: | 0.3 |
| Cholesterol (mg): | 68.4 | Bread: | 0.0 |
| Sodium (mg): | 376 | Meat: | 3.0 |
| % Calories from fat: | 32 | Fat: | 1.0 |

# AROUND-THE-WORLD DRUMSTICKS

### Serves 9 *(2 drumsticks per person)*

1½ teaspoons ground ginger
1½ teaspoons ground coriander
1½ teaspoons ground allspice
  1 teaspoon cinnamon
  1 teaspoon red pepper flakes
  ½ teaspoon salt
  ¼ cup rice wine, *or* sake
  3 tablespoons low-sodium soy sauce
  3 tablespoons sesame oil
  1 tablespoon sugar
  1 tablespoon ginger, minced
  1 tablespoon garlic, minced
 18 chicken drumsticks, skin and fat removed
    Non-stick cooking spray

I n dry skillet or wok, stir-fry ground ginger, coriander, allspice, cinnamon, red pepper flakes, and salt over moderate heat 2 minutes. Remove from heat and add wine, soy sauce, sesame oil, sugar, ginger, and garlic; allow to cool.

Place chicken in large plastic bag, add marinade to coat chicken, seal bag, and chill overnight. Discard marinade and grill drumsticks on spray-coated rack, turning frequently, 10-12 minutes until cooked through.

### Nutritional Data

| PER SERVING | | EXCHANGES | |
|---|---|---|---|
| Calories: | 200 | Milk: | 2.7 |
| Fat (gm): | 8.8 | Vegetable: | 0.0 |
| Sat. fat (gm): | 1.7 | Fruit: | 0.1 |
| Cholesterol (mg): | 95.4 | Bread: | 0.0 |
| Sodium (mg): | 379 | Meat: | 0.0 |
| % Calories from fat: | 28 | Fat: | 1.0 |

# NAPA VALLEY BRAISED CHICKEN

### Serves 4

4 boneless chicken breast halves, skin removed
1 tablespoon canola oil
1 clove garlic, minced
2 tablespoons onion, chopped
2 tablespoons flour
2 tablespoons parsley, chopped
Salt, *or* salt substitute, and ground pepper to
taste
1 bay leaf
1 cup white wine
1 cup dry cooking sherry
1 cup white seedless grapes, halved

I n large skillet, brown chicken in oil over medium heat, along with garlic and onion. Stir in flour, parsley, salt, pepper, and bay leaf. Add wine and sherry, bring to low boil, and reduce heat to simmer. Cover and cook 50 minutes. Add grapes and simmer another 10 minutes.

### Nutritional Data

| PER SERVING | | EXCHANGES | |
|---|---|---|---|
| Calories: | 262 | Milk: | 0.0 |
| Fat (gm): | 14.1 | Vegetable: | 0.0 |
| Sat. fat (gm): | 4.4 | Fruit: | 0.5 |
| Cholesterol (mg): | 63 | Bread: | 0.2 |
| Sodium (mg): | 137 | Meat: | 4.0 |
| % Calories from fat: | 24 | Fat: | 2.4 |

# BOB'S KABOBS WITH MINT

### *Serves 6*

¼ cup canola oil
2 tablespoons curry powder
½ teaspoon ground black pepper
½ teaspoon cayenne pepper
3 lbs. boneless chicken breast halves, skin
   removed, meat cut into 1-inch cubes
4 cups fresh mint leaves
4 cups parsley
2 jalapeño peppers, seeded, chopped
1 tablespoon ginger, minced
2 cloves garlic, crushed
2 teaspoons salt, *or* salt substitute
½ cup non-fat plain yogurt
3 tablespoons fresh lemon juice
   Sweetener equivalent to 1 tablespoon sugar
2 red bell peppers, seeded, cut into 1-inch pieces
2 green bell peppers, seeded, cut into 1-in. pcs.
2 small onions, peeled, cut into 1-inch pieces

**M**ix together oil, curry, and black and cayenne pepper in large bowl. Add chicken pieces and marinate in refrigerator 30 or more minutes, stirring every 10 minutes.

In blender or food processor, combine mint, parsley, jalapeño peppers, ginger, garlic, and salt; process until finely chopped. Add yogurt, lemon juice, and sweetener and process until smooth. Transfer to separate serving bowl.

Preheat broiler or grill. Alternate chicken, bell peppers, and onion pieces on skewers. Broil or grill skewers 5-6 minutes per side or until chicken is cooked through. Serve with mint sauce on side.

### *Nutritional Data*

| PER SERVING | | EXCHANGES | |
|---|---|---|---|
| Calories: | 299 | Milk: | 0.1 |
| Fat (gm): | 11.8 | Vegetable: | 0.6 |
| Sat. fat (gm): | 3.4 | Fruit: | 0.0 |
| Cholesterol (mg): | 72.7 | Bread: | 0.0 |
| Sodium (mg): | 159 | Meat: | 3.3 |
| % Calories from fat: | 26 | Fat: | 1.8 |

# CHICKEN GONE NUTS

*Serves 4*

3½ tablespoons shelled pecans, *or* walnuts
2 tablespoons breadcrumbs
4 boneless chicken breast halves, skin removed
1 teaspoon canola oil
   Non-fat cooking spray

**P** reheat broiler or grill. Using food processor or blender, combine nuts and breadcrumbs until finely ground. Place breading in large plastic food storage bag, add each chicken piece separately, and shake until well covered with mixture.

Heat oil in large skillet, and brown chicken over medium heat 1 minute on each side. Transfer chicken breasts to spray-coated broiler pan or grill, and cook another 2 minutes on each side.

---

### Nutritional Data

| PER SERVING | | EXCHANGES | |
|---|---|---|---|
| Calories: | 315 | Milk: | 0.0 |
| Fat (gm): | 19.1 | Vegetable: | 0.0 |
| Sat. fat (gm): | 4.4 | Fruit: | 0.1 |
| Cholesterol (mg): | 0.1 | Bread: | 0.1 |
| Sodium (mg): | 4.1 | Meat: | 4.1 |
| % Calories from fat: | 1 | Fat: | 1.0 |

# CHICKEN FAJITAS IN PITAS

*Serves 4*

6  boneless chicken breast halves, skin removed,
   meat cut into thin strips
1  tablespoon canola oil
   Dash paprika
2  whole pitas, warmed, cut in halves
4  tablespoons salsa
4  tablespoons non-fat sour cream

**H** eat oil in large skillet. Add chicken strips, sprinkle with paprika, and sauté over medium heat, stirring frequently, 4-5 minutes or until chicken is no longer pink inside.

Remove from heat and place ¼ of chicken in each pita pocket. Top with tablespoon of salsa and sour cream and serve.

### *Nutritional Data*

| PER SERVING | | EXCHANGES | |
|---|---|---|---|
| Calories: | 310 | Milk: | 0.1 |
| Fat (gm): | 13.8 | Vegetable: | 0.1 |
| Sat. fat (gm): | 3.4 | Fruit: | 0.0 |
| Cholesterol (mg): | 69.6 | Bread: | 1.0 |
| Sodium (mg): | 269 | Meat: | 3.0 |
| % Calories from fat: | 28 | Fat: | 0.7 |

# CHICKEN ROMANOV

***Serves 4***

4 boneless chicken breast halves, skin removed,
   meat cut into strips
2 tablespoons canola oil
1 cup onion, chopped
4 tablespoons flour
1¾ cups defatted chicken stock
½ cup non-fat sour cream

 eat oil in large skillet. Add onion and cook over medium heat 2-3 minutes until tender. Remove onion and set aside.

Add chicken strips and sauté 4-5 minutes until tender. Sprinkle with flour and stir well in skillet. Gradually add stock, stirring until smooth. Add onion and cook until thickened, stirring occasionally.

Reduce heat, add sour cream, and heat through. Do *not* bring to boil. Serve immediately.

***Nutritional Data***

| PER SERVING | | EXCHANGES | |
|---|---|---|---|
| Calories: | 263 | Milk: | 0.3 |
| Fat (gm): | 9.3 | Vegetable: | 0.5 |
| Sat. fat (gm): | 3 | Fruit: | 0.0 |
| Cholesterol (mg): | 46.4 | Bread: | 0.4 |
| Sodium (mg): | 407 | Meat: | 2.0 |
| % Calories from fat: | 29 | Fat: | 1.3 |

# CHICKEN MADRID

**Serves 4**

6 chicken legs or thighs, skin removed
1 tablespoon canola oil
1 small onion, sliced
1 14½-oz. can stewed tomatoes, with juice
½ of 15-oz. can artichoke hearts, drained
Salt, *or* salt substitute, and ground pepper to
taste

H eat oil in large skillet. Brown chicken over medium heat 2-3 minutes per side; then remove. Add onion to skillet and cook 2 minutes. Add tomatoes, artichokes, salt, and pepper. Return chicken to skillet, cover, and simmer 45 minutes.

### Nutritional Data

| PER SERVING | | EXCHANGES | |
|---|---|---|---|
| Calories: | 328 | Milk: | 0.0 |
| Fat (gm): | 19.2 | Vegetable: | 1.9 |
| Sat. fat (gm): | 7.2 | Fruit: | 0.0 |
| Cholesterol (mg): | 119 | Bread: | 0.0 |
| Sodium (mg): | 404 | Meat: | 3.5 |
| % Calories from fat: | 28 | Fat: | 3.7 |

# SANTA FE CHICKEN OLÉ

### Serves 6

6  boneless chicken breast halves, skin removed
2  teaspoons ground cumin, divided
1  teaspoon garlic salt
1  tablespoon canola oil
1  cup cooked, *or* canned, black beans, rinsed, drained
1  cup frozen corn
2/3  cup picante sauce
1/2  cup red bell pepper, diced
2  tablespoons cilantro, chopped

S eason chicken with 1 teaspoon cumin and garlic salt. Heat oil in skillet, add chicken, and cook over medium heat 3-4 minutes.

In separate bowl, combine beans, corn, picante sauce, bell pepper, and remaining cumin. Spoon mixture over chicken and cook, uncovered, 6-7 more minutes at reduced heat.

Remove chicken to platter, but leave bean mixture in skillet. Cook beans on high heat another 2-3 minutes, stirring frequently. Spread bean mixture over chicken, top with cilantro, and serve with extra picante sauce on the side.

### Nutritional Data

| PER SERVING | | EXCHANGES | |
|---|---|---|---|
| Calories: | 212 | Milk: | 0.0 |
| Fat (gm): | 9.3 | Vegetable: | 0.6 |
| Sat. fat (gm): | 2.3 | Fruit: | 0.0 |
| Cholesterol (mg): | 46.7 | Bread: | 0.7 |
| Sodium (mg): | 711 | Meat: | 2.1 |
| % Calories from fat: | 29 | Fat: | 0.4 |

# HEARTY CHICKEN AND LENTILS

---

*Serves 7*

4 slices turkey bacon, *or* vegetarian bacon, cut
  into 2-inch pieces
3 tablespoons olive oil
2½ lbs. fryer chicken, cut into pieces, skin
  removed
1 cup dried lentils
1 large stalk celery, cut into 1-inch pieces
1 medium onion, chopped
1 large clove garlic, minced
½ cup dry white wine
1 16-oz. can chopped tomatoes, with liquid
1 teaspoon salt
½ teaspoon dried thyme
1 tablespoon fresh parsley, chopped

I n large skillet, fry turkey bacon in olive oil until crisp, then
remove. Brown chicken over medium heat in combination of bacon
"drippings," remaining oil, and chicken's own juices. Remove chicken and
set aside.

    Add lentils, celery, onion, garlic, wine, tomatoes with juice, salt,
thyme, and reserved turkey bacon to skillet. Place chicken on top of mixture and simmer, covered, 45 minutes. Garnish with parsley.

---

### Nutritional Data

| PER SERVING | | EXCHANGES | |
|---|---|---|---|
| Calories: | 318 | Milk: | 0.0 |
| Fat (gm): | 19 | Vegetable: | 0.5 |
| Sat. fat (gm): | 5.9 | Fruit: | 0.0 |
| Cholesterol (mg): | 100 | Bread: | 1.1 |
| Sodium (mg): | 594 | Meat: | 4.9 |
| % Calories from fat: | 28 | Fat: | 0.5 |

# ROYAL PALACE CHICKEN AND POTATOES

### Serves 4

1 lb. potatoes, peeled, cut into large chunks
2 tablespoons milk
2 tablespoons diet margarine
½ teaspoon salt
   Dash ground white pepper
1 egg yolk, beaten
¼ cup flour
1 teaspoon salt
½ teaspoon paprika
⅛ teaspoon ground black pepper
7 chicken drumsticks, skin removed
2 tablespoons canola oil
½ cup dry white wine
¼ cup water
4 ozs. pearl onions, peeled
2 medium carrots, peeled, cut into thin strips
¼ teaspoon dried thyme
¼ teaspoon salt
1 tablespoon diet margarine, melted

I n large saucepan, heat 1 inch of salted water to boiling. Add potatoes, cover, and simmer 20-25 minutes. Drain water from pan. Mash potatoes until lumps are gone, gradually beating in milk. Add diet margarine, ½ teaspoon salt, and white pepper; then beat until potatoes are light and fluffy. Beat in egg yolk.

Drop mixture by spoonfuls on ungreased cookie sheet and refrigerate.

Mix ¼ cup flour, 1 teaspoon salt, paprika, and black pepper and coat chicken pieces. Heat oil in large skillet and brown chicken on all sides over medium heat, about 15 minutes. Remove drumsticks from skillet.

Add wine, water, onions, carrots, thyme, and ¼ teaspoon salt to skillet. Cover and simmer 10 minutes. Return drumsticks, cover, and simmer 30-40 minutes until chicken is cooked through.

Preheat oven to 425 degrees. Remove potatoes from refrigerator, brush with melted diet margarine, and heat in oven 15 minutes. Serve potatoes with chicken.

### *Nutritional Data*

| PER SERVING | | EXCHANGES | |
|---|---|---|---|
| Calories: | 369 | Milk: | 0.0 |
| Fat (gm): | 21 | Vegetable: | 0.3 |
| Sat. fat (gm): | 3 | Fruit: | 0.0 |
| Cholesterol (mg): | 99.4 | Bread: | 1.6 |
| Sodium (mg): | 534 | Meat: | 2.5 |
| % Calories from fat: | 21 | Fat: | 3.6 |

# CANCUN CHICKEN LOAF

*Serves 4*

1 lb. extra-lean chicken, ground
¼ cup uncooked rolled oats
½ cup onion, minced
   Dash garlic powder
⅛ teaspoon ground coriander
⅛ teaspoon dried thyme, crushed
4 tablespoons low-sodium tomato sauce
1 egg, beaten
1 tablespoon toasted sunflower seeds
3 tablespoons canned green chili peppers, diced
   Non-stick cooking spray

P reheat oven to 350 degrees. Mix together all ingredients and shape into loaf. Place in glass baking dish that has been coated with non-stick spray. Bake 1 hour.

## Nutritional Data

| PER SERVING | | EXCHANGES | |
|---|---|---|---|
| Calories: | 254 | Milk: | 0.0 |
| Fat (gm): | 13.3 | Vegetable: | 0.6 |
| Sat. fat (gm): | 3.1 | Fruit: | 0.6 |
| Cholesterol (mg): | 100 | Bread: | 0.2 |
| Sodium (mg): | 166 | Meat: | 3.5 |
| % Calories from fat: | 28 | Fat: | 0.4 |

# CHICKEN BURRITOS WITH A BITE

### Serves 8

1 tablespoon canola oil
1 lb. ground chicken
⅛ teaspoon ground cumin
⅛ teaspoon garlic powder
⅛ teaspoon dried basil, crushed
1 cup onion, chopped
1 16-oz. can pinto beans, drained and rinsed
4 tablespoons canned green chili peppers, chopped
8 flour tortillas
 Non-stick cooking spray
½ cup low-fat Cheddar cheese, shredded
 Taco sauce

**P**reheat oven to 325 degrees. Heat oil in large skillet over medium heat. Add chicken, cumin, garlic, basil, and onion. Brown chicken, stirring often. Add beans and chili peppers.

Wrap tortillas together in aluminum foil, heat in oven 10-12 minutes, and remove. Increase oven temperature to 350 degrees. Place a portion of chicken mixture on top of each tortilla, roll up, and tuck in edges.

Place tortillas in baking dish (sprayed with non-stick spray), sprinkle with cheese, and bake 15 minutes. Serve with taco sauce.

### Nutritional Data

| PER SERVING | | EXCHANGES | |
|---|---|---|---|
| Calories: | 292 | Milk: | 0.0 |
| Fat (gm): | 10.2 | Vegetable: | 0.3 |
| Sat. fat (gm): | 2.5 | Fruit: | 0.0 |
| Cholesterol (mg): | 37.8 | Bread: | 1.8 |
| Sodium (mg): | 498 | Meat: | 1.9 |
| % Calories from fat: | 32 | Fat: | 0.6 |

# CHICKEN CALZONI BELISSIMO

◆

**Serves 8** *(½ pastry per person)*

**Pastry**

1 pkg. active dry yeast
1 cup warm water
1 tablespoon sugar
2 tablespoons shortening
1 small egg
1 teaspoon salt
4 cups flour, divided
  Non-stick cooking spray

**D**issolve yeast in warm water. Add sugar, shortening, egg, salt, and half of flour. Beat until smooth. Mix in rest of flour. Divide into 4 balls. Put into sprayed bowl, cover with plastic wrap, and set aside.

**Filling**

½ tablespoon olive oil
½ cup onion, chopped
¾ lb. chicken, ground
¼ teaspoon garlic powder
½ teaspoon dried basil, crushed
½ teaspoon dried marjoram, crushed
¼ teaspoon dried thyme, crushed
¼ teaspoon dried oregano, crushed
1½ cups fresh mushrooms, sliced
16 ozs. low-fat, low-sodium mozzarella cheese, shredded
⅛ cup Parmesan cheese, grated
  Cornmeal

Heat oil in skillet and sauté onion over medium heat 2 minutes. Add chicken, garlic, basil, marjoram, thyme, and oregano. Cook until chicken is no longer pink. Add mushrooms and cook 2 minutes more. Add mozzarella cheese and cook just until slightly melted.

On a floured surface, roll out one of the 4 balls of dough to an 11-inch round. Spread ¼ of filling on half of dough round. Fold other half of dough over chicken, press edges together, and crimp. Repeat with remaining dough rounds.

Preheat oven to 425 degrees. Spray cookie sheet with non-stick spray, sprinkle calzones with Parmesan and cornmeal, and bake 15-20 minutes. Serve with Tomato Sauce (see recipe below).

### Tomato Sauce

   2 8-oz. cans low-sodium tomato sauce
   ½ teaspoon dried thyme, crushed
   ½ teaspoon dried marjoram, crushed
   ⅛ teaspoon garlic powder
   ¼ teaspoon water

Combine all ingredients in saucepan, and simmer 15-20 minutes.

---

### Nutritional Data

| PER SERVING | | EXCHANGES | |
|---|---|---|---|
| Calories: | 395 | Milk: | 0.0 |
| Fat (gm): | 13.7 | Vegetable: | 1.1 |
| Sat. fat (gm): | 5 | Fruit: | 0.3 |
| Cholesterol (mg): | 75.9 | Bread: | 2.8 |
| Sodium (mg): | 776 | Meat: | 3.4 |
| % Calories from fat: | 28 | Fat: | 1.5 |

# OLD-FASHIONED CHICKEN SAUSAGE DINNER

*Serves 4*

1 tablespoon canola oil
½ cup green bell pepper, minced
½ cup onion, minced
1¼ lbs. chicken, ground
¼ teaspoon ground sage
¼ teaspoon dried thyme
¼ teaspoon dried marjoram
⅛ teaspoon ground savory
¼ teaspoon ground black pepper
½ teaspoon fennel seeds, crushed
¼ teaspoon salt, *or* salt substitute

H eat oil in large skillet and cook peppers and onion over medium heat 8-10 minutes. Remove from skillet and combine in large bowl with chicken and remaining seasonings. Refrigerate 1 hour.

Divide mixture and form into 8 thin patties. Cook in non-stick skillet over low heat until browned on each side.

### Nutritional Data

| PER SERVING | | EXCHANGES | |
|---|---|---|---|
| Calories: | 289 | Milk: | 0.0 |
| Fat (gm): | 16.6 | Vegetable: | 0.5 |
| Sat. fat (gm): | 4.2 | Fruit: | 0.0 |
| Cholesterol (mg): | 90.7 | Bread: | 0.0 |
| Sodium (mg): | 91 | Meat: | 3.9 |
| % Calories from fat: | 23 | Fat: | 0.7 |

# PASTA WITH CHICKEN MARINARA

***Serves 8***

  2 tablespoons olive oil, divided
  2 cups onion, chopped
1½ cups celery, chopped
  1 clove garlic, minced
  1 lb. chicken, ground
  ½ teaspoon salt, *or* salt substitute
  ¼ teaspoon ground black pepper
  ¾ teaspoon dried basil, crushed
  ⅛ teaspoon dried rosemary, crushed
  ¼ teaspoon dried thyme, crushed
  2 16-oz. cans crushed tomatoes
  2 cups zucchini, chopped
16 ozs. cooked linguine

**H**eat 1½ tablespoons oil in large, heavy saucepan. Add onion, celery, and garlic and sauté over medium heat 4-5 minutes. Remove from pan.

Add and heat remaining ½ tablespoon oil. Add chicken, salt or salt substitute, pepper, basil, rosemary, and thyme. Brown chicken, stirring well.

Return onion and celery to pan. Add tomatoes with juice and zucchini; bring to boil. Cover and simmer 25-30 minutes, stirring frequently. Uncover and continue simmering until thickened, another 20 minutes. Serve over pasta.

***Nutritional Data***

| PER SERVING | | EXCHANGES | |
|---|---|---|---|
| Calories: | 376 | Milk: | 0.0 |
| Fat (gm): | 9.8 | Vegetable: | 1.4 |
| Sat. fat (gm): | 2.1 | Fruit: | 0.0 |
| Cholesterol (mg): | 36.3 | Bread: | 2.0 |
| Sodium (mg): | 242 | Meat: | 1.6 |
| % Calories from fat: | 24 | Fat: | 0.7 |

# FLORIDA CHICKEN À L'ORANGE

### Serves 6

1 8-oz. can low-sodium tomato sauce
3 tablespoons reduced-calorie orange mar-
   malade
1 teaspoon white vinegar
⅛ teaspoon garlic powder
1 tablespoon dried onion flakes
1 teaspoon Worcestershire sauce
   Salt, *or* salt substitute, and ground pepper
   to taste
2 lbs. boneless chicken parts, skin removed
   Non-stick cooking spray

**P**reheat oven to 350 degrees. Combine all ingredients except chicken in small bowl. Allow to stand 15-20 minutes.

Place chicken in baking pan coated with non-stick spray. Spread half of sauce over chicken and bake, uncovered, 1 hour, basting several times. Heat remaining sauce and serve with chicken.

### Nutritional Data

| PER SERVING | | EXCHANGES | |
|---|---|---|---|
| Calories: | 298 | Milk: | 0.0 |
| Fat (gm): | 14 | Vegetable: | 0.5 |
| Sat. fat (gm): | 4 | Fruit: | 0.4 |
| Cholesterol (mg): | 96.8 | Bread: | 0.0 |
| Sodium (mg): | 119 | Meat: | 4.2 |
| % Calories from fat: | 23 | Fat: | 0.0 |

# FAMILY FAVORITE CHICKEN

**Serves 4**

- 1 8-oz. can low-sodium tomato sauce
- 2 tablespoons dried onion flakes
- 1 packet instant beef-flavored broth mix
- ½ cup water
- 1¼ lbs. boneless chicken parts, skin removed
- Non-stick cooking spray

P reheat oven to 350 degrees. Combine tomato sauce, onion, beef broth mix, and water in small bowl. Place chicken in baking pan sprayed with non-stick spray. Pour tomato mixture over chicken and bake, covered, 30 minutes. Remove cover and bake an additional 30 minutes.

### Nutritional Data

| PER SERVING | | EXCHANGES | |
|---|---|---|---|
| Calories: | 270 | Milk: | 0.0 |
| Fat (gm): | 13.3 | Vegetable: | 0.9 |
| Sat. fat (gm): | 3.8 | Fruit: | 0.0 |
| Cholesterol (mg): | 90.9 | Bread: | 0.0 |
| Sodium (mg): | 357 | Meat: | 3.9 |
| % Calories from fat: | 29 | Fat: | 0.0 |

# CHICKEN MINI PIES

*Serves 4*

2 tablespoons diet margarine
4 tablespoons onion, chopped
4 tablespoons flour
2 teaspoons instant chicken bouillon granules
¼ teaspoon ground sage
   Dash ground pepper
1⅓ cups skim milk
1 cup water
1 cup cooked boneless, skinless chicken, ground
1 cup frozen mixed vegetables
2 tablespoons parsley, chopped
1 pkg. (6) refrigerated biscuits

**P** reheat oven to 400 degrees. Heat diet margarine in large skillet. Cook onion 3-4 minutes over medium heat until tender. Add flour, bouillon, sage, and pepper, stirring constantly. Gradually add milk and water. Cook, stirring constantly, until thickened.

Add chicken, vegetables, and parsley and heat until mixture is consistency of stew. Remove from heat and pour into 4 individual casseroles.

Top each casserole with 1 biscuit. (Reserve and refrigerate remaining 2 biscuits for other use.) Place casseroles on baking sheet, and bake 10-12 minutes until biscuits are lightly browned.

### Nutritional Data

| PER SERVING | | EXCHANGES | |
|---|---|---|---|
| Calories: | 387 | Milk: | 0.3 |
| Fat (gm): | 19.1 | Vegetable: | 1.0 |
| Sat. fat (gm): | 5.3 | Fruit: | 0.0 |
| Cholesterol (mg): | 65 | Bread: | 0.4 |
| Sodium (mg): | 736 | Meat: | 2.9 |
| % Calories from fat: | 20 | Fat: | 1.2 |

# POTLUCK CHICKEN

**Serves 8**

4 cups cooked boneless chicken, skin removed,
  meat diced
2 cups white rice, cooked
2 cups wild rice, cooked
1 can cream of celery soup
1 medium jar pimiento, diced
2 cups frozen French-style green beans
1 cup non-fat mayonnaise
1 small can water chestnuts, drained, diced
1 medium onion, chopped

reheat oven to 350 degrees. Combine all ingredients. Bake in
3-quart casserole 35 minutes.

## Nutritional Data

| PER SERVING | | EXCHANGES | |
|---|---|---|---|
| Calories: | 348 | Milk: | 0.0 |
| Fat (gm): | 11.5 | Vegetable: | 0.7 |
| Sat. fat (gm): | 3.3 | Fruit: | 0.0 |
| Cholesterol (mg): | 74.3 | Bread: | 1.4 |
| Sodium (mg): | 527 | Meat: | 3.1 |
| % Calories from fat: | 30 | Fat: | 0.1 |

# MIDDLE EASTERN CHICKEN CASSEROLE

*Serves 8*

Non-stick cooking spray
1 10- to 12-oz. can artichoke hearts, drained, quartered
1 15-oz. can chickpeas, drained
1 15-oz. can chopped tomatoes with juice
3 carrots, peeled, chopped
¾ cup defatted chicken stock
1 tablespoon fresh or dried mint leaves, chopped
1 teaspoon garlic, chopped
1 cup medium bulgur, uncooked
1 tablespoon lemon peel, finely grated
2 tablespoons cornstarch
4 tablespoons cold water
1 2½-lb. chicken, cut into pieces, skin removed
¼ cup parsley, chopped
¼ cup cucumber, chopped

P reheat oven to 350 degrees. Lightly coat large casserole with non-stick cooking spray. Combine artichokes, chickpeas, tomatoes, carrots, chicken stock, mint, garlic, bulgur, and lemon peel and pour into casserole.

In separate bowl, mix together cornstarch and water until smooth. Add to vegetable mixture, and mix well. Place chicken pieces on top of vegetables.

Cover and bake 45 minutes. Remove cover and bake another 15 minutes. Sprinkle with parsley and cucumber before serving.

## Nutritional Data

| PER SERVING | | EXCHANGES | |
|---|---|---|---|
| Calories: | 323 | Milk: | 0.0 |
| Fat (gm): | 14.8 | Vegetable: | 1.2 |
| Sat. fat (gm): | 4.3 | Fruit: | 0.0 |
| Cholesterol (mg): | 100 | Bread: | 1.7 |
| Sodium (mg): | 214 | Meat: | 4.1 |
| % Calories from fat: | 30 | Fat: | 0.0 |

# BANGKOK BAKED CHICKEN

*Serves 7*

¾ cup regular milk
¼ cup garlic, minced
⅛ cup ginger, minced
⅛ cup olive oil
1 tablespoon low-sodium soy sauce
1 tablespoon curry powder
1½ teaspoons ground black pepper
1½ teaspoons ground white pepper
Sweetener equivalent to 1½ teaspoons sugar
½ teaspoon turmeric
2½ lbs. chicken, cut up, skin removed
4 slices fresh pineapple
**Sweet-Hot sauce** (see recipe below)

**I**n large bowl, combine all ingredients except chicken, pineapple, and Sweet-Hot Sauce. Add chicken pieces and mix well. Cover bowl with plastic wrap and refrigerate to marinate overnight.

Preheat oven to 350 degrees. Remove chicken from marinade and bake 45 minutes, basting 2-3 times with marinade. Garnish with pineapple and Sweet-Hot Sauce.

*Sweet-Hot Sauce*

¼ teaspoon flour
1½ teaspoons cold water
¼ cup rice vinegar
Sweetener equivalent to ⅛ cup sugar
1 tablespoon plum sauce
1½ teaspoons low-sodium soy sauce
1½ teaspoons lime juice
1 teaspoon low-sodium tomato paste
½ teaspoon garlic, minced
¼ teaspoon chili pepper, minced
¼ teaspoon ground red chili paste
¼ teaspoon paprika
¼ teaspoon salt, *or* salt substitute

Mix together flour and water in small saucepan. Add all remaining ingredients, and bring to boil. Reduce heat and simmer 4 minutes. Cool and serve with Bangkok Baked Chicken.

### Nutritional Data

| PER SERVING | | EXCHANGES | |
|---|---|---|---|
| Calories: | 299 | Milk: | 0.1 |
| Fat (gm): | 23.7 | Vegetable: | 0.0 |
| Sat. fat (gm): | 6 | Fruit: | 0.2 |
| Cholesterol (mg): | 94 | Bread: | 0.0 |
| Sodium (mg): | 503 | Meat: | 5.0 |
| % Calories from fat: | 30 | Fat: | 1.7 |

# ONION "FRIED" CHICKEN

### Serves 4

4 boneless chicken breast halves, skin removed
  Non-stick cooking spray
2 tablespoons non-fat mayonnaise
2 tablespoons corn flakes, crushed
2 tablespoons dried onion flakes
1 packet instant beef-flavored broth mix

**P**reheat oven to 350 degrees. Spray shallow baking dish with cooking spray, and place chicken in dish. Brush chicken pieces with mayonnaise.

Mix remaining ingredients in separate bowl, and sprinkle over chicken. Press mixture into mayonnaise coating. Bake, uncovered, 45 minutes.

### Nutritional Data

| PER SERVING | | EXCHANGES | |
|---|---|---|---|
| Calories: | 127 | Milk: | 0.0 |
| Fat (gm): | 4.1 | Vegetable: | 0.0 |
| Sat. fat (gm): | 1.8 | Fruit: | 0.1 |
| Cholesterol (mg): | 43.3 | Bread: | 0.8 |
| Sodium (mg): | 385 | Meat: | 2.0 |
| % Calories from fat: | 30 | Fat: | 0.0 |

# AUTUMN APPLE CHICKEN

**Serves 4**

- 1 cup low-sugar applesauce
- ½ cup low-sodium soy sauce
- 1½ cloves garlic, minced
- ½ teaspoon ground ginger
- ½ teaspoon sugar substitute (optional)
- 3 drops chili sauce, *or* Tabasco
- 1 lb. chicken pieces, skin and bones removed, ground

C ombine all ingredients except chicken. Pour marinade over chicken and refrigerate overnight. Drain meat mixture well and pat dry with paper towel before placing in baking pan. Reserve marinade.

Preheat oven to 350 degrees. Bake, covered with foil, 1 hour. Uncover and baste with marinade; bake 15 minutes more. Turn pieces, baste again, and bake an additional 15 minutes before serving.

### Nutritional Data

| PER SERVING | | EXCHANGES | |
|---|---|---|---|
| Calories: | 287 | Milk: | 0.0 |
| Fat (gm): | 17 | Vegetable: | 0.0 |
| Sat. fat (gm): | 5.1 | Fruit: | 0.5 |
| Cholesterol (mg): | 100 | Bread: | 0.0 |
| Sodium (mg): | 766 | Meat: | 4.2 |
| % Calories from fat: | 29 | Fat: | 0.0 |

# CALIFORNIA CHICKEN CASSEROLE

### Serves 4

1 tablespoon canola oil
1 tablespoon fresh thyme, chopped, *or* 1
   teaspoon dried
4 boneless chicken breast halves, skin removed
½ teaspoon ground black pepper, divided
½ cup onion, minced
2 garlic cloves, minced
1 red bell pepper, seeded, cut into strips
1 15-oz. can artichoke hearts, drained
2 tablespoons dry white wine
¼ teaspoon salt, *or* salt substitute

**P**reheat oven to 375 degrees.

   In medium skillet, heat oil and thyme. Add chicken breasts, sprinkle with ¼ teaspoon pepper, and brown over medium heat 1 minute. Turn chicken over, sprinkle with remaining pepper, and cook another 1 minute. Remove chicken from pan.

   Add onion and garlic to cooking juices in skillet, and sauté 1 minute. Add bell pepper, artichokes, wine, and salt; cook another 1 minute.

   Spoon half of vegetables into 8-inch casserole, add chicken breasts, and cover with remaining vegetables. Bake, uncovered, 20 minutes.

### Nutritional Data

| PER SERVING | | EXCHANGES | |
|---|---|---|---|
| Calories: | 215 | Milk: | 0.0 |
| Fat (gm): | 10.7 | Vegetable: | 0.2 |
| Sat. fat (gm): | 2.5 | Fruit: | 0.0 |
| Cholesterol (mg): | 46.4 | Bread: | 0.0 |
| Sodium (mg): | 103 | Meat: | 2.0 |
| % Calories from fat: | 27 | Fat: | 0.8 |

# HILLBILLY CHICKEN BAKE

### Serves 8

1 fryer chicken, cut into small pieces, skin and
  bones removed
  Non-stick cooking spray
2 cans low-sodium, low-fat cream of chicken
  soup, divided
⅔ cup water, divided
½ teaspoon ground ginger
1 cup Bisquick, *or* other baking mix
¼ cup yellow cornmeal

**P** reheat oven to 350 degrees.

Place chicken in 3-quart casserole coated with cooking spray. Combine 1½ cans soup, ⅓ cup water, and ginger. Add mixture to casserole, cover, and bake 60 minutes.

Meanwhile, combine remaining ingredients. Remove casserole. Drop about 8 mounds of dough over chicken, and return to 450-degree oven. Bake, uncovered, 15 minutes more or until biscuits are golden.

### Nutritional Data

| PER SERVING | | EXCHANGES | |
|---|---|---|---|
| Calories: | 327 | Milk: | 0.0 |
| Fat (gm): | 13 | Vegetable: | 0.0 |
| Sat. fat (gm): | 4 | Fruit: | 0.0 |
| Cholesterol (mg): | 79 | Bread: | 2.0 |
| Sodium (mg): | 779 | Meat: | 3.2 |
| % Calories from fat: | 28 | Fat: | 0.7 |

# 8.
# THE QUICK CHICKEN
*Salads and Meals in a Hurry*

# DYNAMITE CHICKEN DIP

**Serves 20**

1 cup cooked boneless chicken, skin removed,
   meat cubed
1 8-oz. package non-fat cream cheese, softened
2 8-oz. jars light Cheese Whiz
1 cup medium salsa
1 4-oz. can green chilies, diced

**C** ombine ingredients in medium saucepan. Cook over medium heat, stirring constantly, until smooth. Transfer ingredients to microwave dish, cover, and microwave on Medium-High 3-4 minutes, stirring every 30 seconds. Serve hot dip with low-fat crackers.

## Nutritional Data

| PER SERVING | | EXCHANGES | |
|---|---|---|---|
| Calories: | 115 | Milk: | 0.2 |
| Fat (gm): | 7.9 | Vegetable: | 0.2 |
| Sat. fat (gm): | 4.6 | Fruit: | 0.0 |
| Cholesterol (mg): | 26.2 | Bread: | 0.0 |
| Sodium (mg): | 458 | Meat: | 0.8 |
| % Calories from fat: | 22 | Fat: | 1.1 |

# CHUNKY CHICKEN DIP

### *Serves 8*

1 15-oz. can artichoke hearts, drained, chopped
1½ cups Parmesan cheese, grated
2 cups non-fat mayonnaise
4 ozs. fresh, mild green chilies, diced
1½ cups cooked boneless chicken, skin removed,
meat cubed

ombine all ingredients in small saucepan, and cook over low heat until heated through. Do *not* boil. Serve warm with crackers or Melba toast.

### *Nutritional Data*

| PER SERVING | | EXCHANGES | |
|---|---|---|---|
| Calories: | 199 | Milk: | 0.0 |
| Fat (gm): | 9.4 | Vegetable: | 1.1 |
| Sat. fat (gm): | 3.2 | Fruit: | 5.9 |
| Cholesterol (mg): | 41 | Bread: | 0.0 |
| Sodium (mg): | 583 | Meat: | 2.7 |
| % Calories from fat: | 30 | Fat: | 0.8 |

# HONEY DRUMSTICKS

**Serves 8**

4 chicken legs with thighs, skin removed, cut in half

¼ teaspoon ground black pepper

1 teaspoon salt, *or* salt substitute

1 tablespoon honey

1 teaspoon Worcestershire sauce

¼ teaspoon dry mustard

¼ cup orange juice

**P** reheat oven to 375 degrees.

Place chicken in shallow baking dish. Sprinkle liberally with salt (or salt substitute) and pepper. Bake 30 minutes.

Combine remaining ingredients and brush over drumsticks. Bake and baste another 20 minutes.

### *Nutritional Data*

| PER SERVING | | EXCHANGES | |
|---|---|---|---|
| Calories: | 111 | Milk: | 0.0 |
| Fat (gm): | 7.1 | Vegetable: | 0.0 |
| Sat. fat (gm): | 2.1 | Fruit: | 0.2 |
| Cholesterol (mg): | 39 | Bread: | 0.0 |
| Sodium (mg): | 43.1 | Meat: | 1.6 |
| % Calories from fat: | 15 | Fat: | 1.0 |

# MONDAY NIGHT FOOTBALL "WINGS"

*Serves 16*

16 chicken thighs, boneless, cut in half
½ cup low-sodium soy sauce
Juice of 2 lemons
Sweetener equivalent to ½ cup sugar

P lace thighs in shallow baking dish. Combine all remaining ingredients and pour over wings. Marinate for 1 hour, turning chicken 3-4 times. Broil or grill 5-6 minutes per side.

## Nutritional Data

| PER SERVING | | EXCHANGES | |
|---|---|---|---|
| Calories: | 103 | Milk: | 0.0 |
| Fat (gm): | 9.3 | Vegetable: | 0.0 |
| Sat. fat (gm): | 4.1 | Fruit: | 0.0 |
| Cholesterol (mg): | 79 | Bread: | 0.0 |
| Sodium (mg): | 326 | Meat: | 2.3 |
| % Calories from fat: | 15 | Fat: | 1.5 |

# MELON BALL CHICKEN SALAD

**Serves 6**

2 cups cooked boneless chicken, skin removed,
  meat diced
2 stalks celery, diced
4 tablespoons fresh parsley, minced
2 cups honeydew melon balls
2 cups cantaloupe balls
²/₃ cup non-fat mayonnaise
²/₃ cup non-fat sour cream
  Juice of 1 lime
2 teaspoons honey
1 tablespoon fresh ginger, minced
  Salt, *or* salt substitute, and ground pepper
  to taste
6 large (or 12 small) lettuce leaves

I n large bowl, combine chicken, celery, parsley, and melon balls. In separate bowl, whisk together mayonnaise, sour cream, lime, honey, ginger, salt (or salt substitute), and pepper. Add dressing to chicken mixture, and coat well. Serve on lettuce leaves.

### Nutritional Data

| PER SERVING | | EXCHANGES | |
|---|---|---|---|
| Calories: | 210 | Milk: | 0.2 |
| Fat (gm): | 7.3 | Vegetable: | 0.0 |
| Sat. fat (gm): | 2.2 | Fruit: | 1.1 |
| Cholesterol (mg): | 48.4 | Bread: | 0.0 |
| Sodium (mg): | 402 | Meat: | 2.1 |
| % Calories from fat: | 31 | Fat: | 0.0 |

# CHICKEN AND WILD RICE SALAD

*Serves 6*

1¼ cups wild rice, rinsed
3¼ cups water
1 teaspoon salt, *or* salt substitute
½ tablespoon white wine vinegar
1 tablespoon olive oil
   Salt, *or* salt substitute, and ground pepper
   to taste
2 whole, smoked boneless chicken breasts, skin
   removed, meat cut into 1-inch pieces
½ bunch green onions, chopped
¼ cup golden raisins
   **Curried Chutney Dressing** (see recipe
   below)
6 large (or 12 small) lettuce leaves

**I**n large saucepan, combine wild rice with water and 1 teaspoon salt (or salt substitute). Bring to boil and reduce to simmer. Cover and cook 45-50 minutes.

Transfer to large bowl, and toss well with vinegar, oil, salt (or salt substitute), and pepper. Allow to cool.

Add chicken, green onions, raisins and Curried Chutney Dressing (see recipe below); mix well to coat. Serve on lettuce leaves.

*Curried Chutney Dressing*

1 clove garlic, minced
1 tablespoon white wine vinegar
2 tablespoons fresh lemon juice
¾ tablespoon curry powder
1½ tablespoons bottled mango chutney
⅓ cup olive oil
¼ cup non-fat sour cream
1-2 tablespoons water
¼ cup fresh coriander, minced

In blender or food processor, combine garlic, vinegar, lemon juice, curry powder, and chutney; blend until smooth. With motor running, add oil in stream; then add sour cream and water. Blend until smooth. Stir in coriander before pouring over chicken and rice mixture.

---

### Nutritional Data

| PER SERVING | | EXCHANGES | |
|---|---|---|---|
| Calories: | 287 | Milk: | 0.0 |
| Fat (gm): | 19 | Vegetable: | 0.0 |
| Sat. fat (gm): | 2.7 | Fruit: | 2.3 |
| Cholesterol (mg): | 43 | Bread: | 0.4 |
| Sodium (mg): | 60 | Meat: | 1.8 |
| % Calories from fat: | 30 | Fat: | 2.5 |

# GREEK SMOKED CHICKEN SALAD

***Serves 4***

10 ozs. fresh spinach leaves
1 bunch bok choy, stems trimmed, leaves sliced
6 ozs. boneless smoked chicken, skin removed, meat cut into thin strips
3 turkey bacon, *or* vegetarian bacon slices, cut into ½-inch pieces
6 tablespoons Dijon mustard
2 tablespoons red wine vinegar
5 tablespoons olive oil
2 tablespoons water
4 ozs. low-fat feta cheese, crumbled

**C**ombine spinach, bok choy, and chicken in large bowl and set aside. Cook bacon in large skillet until crisp; remove, drain, and discard skillet drippings.

Using very low heat, add mustard and vinegar to skillet, and whisk together until smooth. Whisk in oil and water. Increase heat slightly and add bacon and feta, stirring until heated through, but do *not* boil.

Add enough dressing to greens and chicken to coat salad well. Serve remaining dressing on the side.

***Nutritional Data***

| PER SERVING | | EXCHANGES | |
|---|---|---|---|
| Calories: | 224 | Milk: | 0.0 |
| Fat (gm): | 19.2 | Vegetable: | 0.0 |
| Sat. fat (gm): | 8.5 | Fruit: | 0.0 |
| Cholesterol (mg): | 56.5 | Bread: | 0.0 |
| Sodium (mg): | 418 | Meat: | 1.9 |
| % Calories from fat: | 29 | Fat: | 4.6 |

# CREOLE CHICKEN SALAD

### Serves 4

2 small heads Boston lettuce, torn into pieces
6 plum tomatoes, sliced
2 small onions, sliced
4 teaspoons cayenne
3 teaspoons paprika
2 teaspoons ground black pepper
1 teaspoon chili powder
1 teaspoon garlic powder
1 teaspoon salt substitute
4 boneless chicken breast halves, skin removed
**Louisiana Dressing** (see recipe below)

T oss together lettuce, tomatoes, and onions in large bowl and set aside. Combine spices in small bowl, mixing well. Season both sides of chicken breasts well with spice mixture.

Broil or grill chicken 5-6 minutes per side until cooked through. Allow to cool. Cut into 1-inch pieces and add to vegetables. Pour Louisiana Dressing (see recipe below) over all and toss well.

### Louisiana Dressing

½ cup Dijon mustard
3 tablespoons olive oil
4 tablespoons dry white wine
2 tablespoons honey
Sweetener equivalent to 2 tablespoons sugar
Salt, *or* salt substitute, and ground pepper
to taste

Whisk together all ingredients, and pour over Creole Chicken Salad.

### Nutritional Data

| PER SERVING | | EXCHANGES | |
|---|---|---|---|
| Calories: | 198 | Milk: | 0.0 |
| Fat (gm): | 10.9 | Vegetable: | 0.1 |
| Sat. fat (gm): | 1.6 | Fruit: | 0.5 |
| Cholesterol (mg): | 34.2 | Bread: | 0.1 |
| Sodium (mg): | 40 | Meat: | 1.5 |
| % Calories from fat: | 30 | Fat: | 2.2 |

# WINE COUNTRY CHICKEN SALAD

**Serves 4**

- 3 boneless chicken breast halves, skin removed
- ½ cup non-fat sour cream
- ½ cup plain non-fat yogurt
- ½ cup non-fat mayonnaise
- 1½ cups seedless grapes
- 1 cup celery, diced
- ¼ cup pecan halves
- 2 tablespoons poppy seeds
  Salt, *or* salt substitute, and ground pepper
  to taste

**P**lace chicken in boiling water to cover, and reduce heat to simmer 8-10 minutes. Set aside to cool, then cut into 1-inch pieces.

In separate bowl, whisk together sour cream, yogurt, and mayonnaise. Add chicken and remaining ingredients, tossing well.

### Nutritional Data

| PER SERVING | | EXCHANGES | |
|---|---|---|---|
| Calories: | 205 | Milk: | 0.5 |
| Fat (gm): | 10.3 | Vegetable: | 0.5 |
| Sat. fat (gm): | 1.1 | Fruit: | 0.8 |
| Cholesterol (mg): | 30.8 | Bread: | 0.0 |
| Sodium (mg): | 420 | Meat: | 1.6 |
| % Calories from fat: | 30 | Fat: | 1.9 |

# CHICKEN MACARONI SALAD

*Serves 6*

1½ cups cooked boneless chicken, skin removed,
　　meat cubed
1 cup small macaroni, cooked and drained
3 tomatoes, cubed
1 cup celery, chopped
½ cup red bell pepper, chopped
3 tablespoons green onion, minced
1 teaspoon salt, or salt substitute
½ teaspoon ground black pepper
¼ teaspoon oregano
1 cup defatted chicken stock
1 clove garlic, sliced
¼ cup white wine vinegar

**I**n large bowl, mix together chicken, macaroni, tomatoes, celery, red bell pepper, and green onion. Sprinkle with salt (or salt substitute), pepper, and oregano.

In small saucepan, bring chicken stock and garlic to boil for 10 minutes. Add wine vinegar, mix well, and pour over salad to coat well. Chill and serve.

### Nutritional Data

| PER SERVING | | EXCHANGES | |
|---|---|---|---|
| Calories: | 152 | Milk: | 0.0 |
| Fat (gm): | 1.6 | Vegetable: | 0.0 |
| Sat. fat (gm): | 0.4 | Fruit: | 0.0 |
| Cholesterol (mg): | 49.3 | Bread: | 0.6 |
| Sodium (mg): | 250 | Meat: | 2.2 |
| % Calories from fat: | 10 | Fat: | 0.0 |

# AUTUMN APPLE CHICKEN SALAD

### Serves 4

 2 cups cooked boneless chicken, skin removed, meat cubed
 ½ cup celery, chopped
 ½ cup walnuts, chopped
 1 apple, chopped
 ½ cup low-fat Cheddar cheese, cubed
 ¾ cup non-fat mayonnaise

ombine all ingredients, and mix well. Chill and serve.

### Nutritional Data

| PER SERVING | | EXCHANGES | |
|---|---|---|---|
| Calories: | 297 | Milk: | 0.0 |
| Fat (gm): | 11.8 | Vegetable: | 0.0 |
| Sat. fat (gm): | 1.9 | Fruit: | 0.9 |
| Cholesterol (mg): | 68.7 | Bread: | 0.1 |
| Sodium (mg): | 585 | Meat: | 3.3 |
| % Calories from fat: | 26 | Fat: | 0.0 |

# ESSENTIAL CHICKEN SALAD

### Serves 4

2 cups cooked boneless chicken, skin removed,
    meat cubed
4 tablespoons non-fat mayonnaise
1⅓ cups celery, diced
4 teaspoons lemon juice
2 teaspoons onion powder
4 teaspoons pimiento, diced
1 teaspoon Dijon mustard
⅛ teaspoon dill
⅛ teaspoon sage
    Ground black pepper to taste

ombine all ingredients, and mix well. Chill and serve.

### Nutritional Data

| PER SERVING | | EXCHANGES | |
|---|---|---|---|
| Calories: | 135 | Milk: | 0.0 |
| Fat (gm): | 1.4 | Vegetable: | 0.0 |
| Sat. fat (gm): | 0.4 | Fruit: | 0.2 |
| Cholesterol (mg): | 65.7 | Bread: | 0.0 |
| Sodium (mg): | 243 | Meat: | 2.9 |
| % Calories from fat: | 10 | Fat: | 0.0 |

# CONFETTI CHICKEN SALAD

### Serves 4

 3 medium bell peppers (if possible: 1 yellow, 1 green, 1 red), seeded, cut into strips
 2 cups cooked boneless chicken, skin removed, meat cubed
 1½ cups corn, fresh or frozen, cooked, drained, cooled
 1 green onion, sliced
 2 tablespoons cider vinegar
 1 tablespoon olive oil
 1 tablespoon parsley, chopped
 1 clove garlic, minced
 ½ teaspoon oregano
 Salt, *or* salt substitute, and ground pepper to taste

**C**ombine peppers, chicken, corn, and green onion in large bowl. In separate bowl, whisk together remaining ingredients. Pour over chicken mixture. Chill and serve.

### Nutritional Data

| PER SERVING | | EXCHANGES | |
|---|---|---|---|
| Calories: | 219 | Milk: | 0.0 |
| Fat (gm): | 5.6 | Vegetable: | 0.8 |
| Sat. fat (gm): | 1 | Fruit: | 0.0 |
| Cholesterol (mg): | 65.7 | Bread: | 0.6 |
| Sodium (mg): | 84 | Meat: | 2.9 |
| % Calories from fat: | 22 | Fat: | 0.7 |

# CHICKEN MAJOR GREY SALAD

### Serves 6

6 boneless chicken breast halves, pre-cooked,
  skin removed, meat cubed
½ cup celery, chopped
¼ cup onion, chopped
3 tablespoons chutney
½ cup non-fat mayonnaise
¼ teaspoon curry powder

 n large bowl, combine all ingredients and mix well. Cover and refrigerate 1 hour before serving.

### Nutritional Data

| PER SERVING | | EXCHANGES | |
|---|---|---|---|
| Calories: | 280 | Milk: | 0.0 |
| Fat (gm): | 2.2 | Vegetable: | 0.0 |
| Sat. fat (gm): | 0.6 | Fruit: | 1.4 |
| Cholesterol (mg): | 103 | Bread: | 0.0 |
| Sodium (mg): | 796 | Meat: | 4.5 |
| % Calories from fat: | 7 | Fat: | 0.0 |

# SWEET-AND-SOUR CHICKEN SANDWICHES

### Serves 4

¼ cup low-sodium soy sauce
  Sweetener equivalent to ⅓ cup sugar
¼ cup dry sherry
3 cloves garlic, minced
2 tablespoons fresh ginger, minced
4 boneless chicken breast halves, skin removed
4 whole wheat reduced-calorie hamburger buns
½ avocado, peeled, sliced
  Lettuce
1 large tomato, sliced

I n large bowl, combine soy sauce, sweetener, sherry, garlic, and ginger. Add chicken pieces, and coat well with marinade. Cover and refrigerate 1 hour.

Remove from marinade, and grill or broil chicken 5-6 minutes each side until cooked through. Halve and toast buns. Assemble sandwiches with chicken, then avocado slices, lettuce, and tomato.

### Nutritional Data

| PER SERVING | | EXCHANGES | |
|---|---|---|---|
| Calories: | 212 | Milk: | 0.0 |
| Fat (gm): | 9 | Vegetable: | 0.2 |
| Sat. fat (gm): | 1.2 | Fruit: | 0.2 |
| Cholesterol (mg): | 32.2 | Bread: | 0.7 |
| Sodium (mg): | 800 | Meat: | 1.5 |
| % Calories from fat: | 30 | Fat: | 1.7 |

# APPLE CIDER GRILLED CHICKEN

**Serves 4**

¼ cup apple jelly
4 boneless chicken breast halves, skin removed
¼ cup apple cider vinegar
½ teaspoon salt
½ teaspoon hot pepper sauce
4 reduced-calorie hamburger buns, split

**M**elt jelly in small bowl in microwave, cooking 1 minute on High, or in small saucepan over low heat, stirring often. Add remaining ingredients, except chicken and buns, and mix well.

Grill or broil chicken pieces 5-6 minutes per side, basting several times with dressing. Serve buns and remaining dressing on side.

### Nutritional Data

| PER SERVING | | EXCHANGES | |
|---|---|---|---|
| Calories: | 188 | Milk: | 0.0 |
| Fat (gm): | 2.5 | Vegetable: | 0.0 |
| Sat. fat (gm): | 0.6 | Fruit: | 0.8 |
| Cholesterol (mg): | 34.2 | Bread: | 0.9 |
| Sodium (mg): | 175 | Meat: | 1.5 |
| % Calories from fat: | 12 | Fat: | 0.1 |

# JIFFY CHICKEN BURGERS

***Serves 4***

1¼ lbs. skinless, boneless chicken, ground
3 tablespoons Dijon mustard
3 tablespoons green onions (white part only),
   minced
1 tablespoon low-sodium soy sauce
2 teaspoons Worcestershire sauce
   Salt, *or* salt substitute, and ground pepper
   to taste

**C**ombine all ingredients, mixing lightly, then chill 15 minutes. Form into 4 patties. Broil or grill 5 minutes per side until cooked through.

*Note:* These burgers may tend to fall apart during cooking, so handle carefully.

### Nutritional Data

| PER SERVING | | EXCHANGES | |
|---|---|---|---|
| Calories: | 190 | Milk: | 0.0 |
| Fat (gm): | 2.1 | Vegetable: | 0.0 |
| Sat. fat (gm): | 0.6 | Fruit: | 0.0 |
| Cholesterol (mg): | 98.6 | Bread: | 0.0 |
| Sodium (mg): | 341 | Meat: | 4.3 |
| % Calories from fat: | 11 | Fat: | 0.0 |

# TEXAS CHICKEN BURGERS

*Serves 4*

1 lb. chicken, ground
1 egg white
Salt, *or* salt substitute, and ground pepper
to taste
1 cup low-sodium barbecue sauce
4 slices low-fat Cheddar cheese
4 reduced-calorie hamburger buns, split
1 red onion, sliced

**C**ombine chicken, egg white, salt (or salt substitute), and pepper in small bowl. Mix lightly, then chill 15 minutes. Form into 4 patties. Brush with barbecue sauce, and broil or grill 5 minutes per side until cooked through.

*Note:* These burgers may tend to fall apart during cooking, so handle carefully.

Place cheese slices on burgers during last minute of cooking. Serve on buns with red onion.

### Nutritional Data

| PER SERVING | | EXCHANGES | |
|---|---|---|---|
| Calories: | 233 | Milk: | 0.0 |
| Fat (gm): | 7 | Vegetable: | 1.1 |
| Sat. fat (gm): | 2.1 | Fruit: | 0.2 |
| Cholesterol (mg): | 100 | Bread: | 1.5 |
| Sodium (mg): | 757 | Meat: | 5.3 |
| % Calories from fat: | 17 | Fat: | 0.5 |

# CHINATOWN CHICKEN SANDWICHES

*Serves 4*

1 tablespoon frozen orange juice concentrate
1 tablespoon canola oil
  Sweetener to equal 1 tablespoon sugar
1 tablespoon low-sodium soy sauce
½ teaspoon ground ginger
¼ teaspoon garlic powder
4 boneless chicken breast halves, skin removed
1 medium tomato, sliced
  Alfalfa sprouts
4 reduced-calorie hamburger buns, split

**C**ombine orange juice, oil, sweetener, soy sauce, ginger, and garlic in small bowl. Brush chicken pieces with orange mixture, and broil or grill 5-6 minutes per side, basting twice, until cooked through. Serve on buns with tomato slices and sprouts.

### Nutritional Data

| PER SERVING | | EXCHANGES | |
|---|---|---|---|
| Calories: | 233 | Milk: | 0.0 |
| Fat (gm): | 6.5 | Vegetable: | 0.0 |
| Sat. fat (gm): | 1.2 | Fruit: | 0.1 |
| Cholesterol (mg): | 34.2 | Bread: | 1.5 |
| Sodium (mg): | 493 | Meat: | 1.5 |
| % Calories from fat: | 25 | Fat: | 0.9 |

# Hot Diggity Chickie Pitas

*Serves 4*

4 boneless chicken breast halves, skin removed
Brown sugar low-sodium substitute equivalent
to 3 teaspoons brown sugar
2 teaspoons teriyaki sauce
Juice of 2 limes
2 tablespoons olive oil
1 large, *or* 2 small, red bell peppers, seeded, cut
into strips
2 medium jalapeño peppers, seeded, cut into
strips
Salt, *or* salt substitute, and ground pepper
to taste
2 whole pita breads, cut into halves
**Refreshing Dressing** (see recipe below)

C ombine brown sugar substitute, teriyaki sauce, and lime juice in large bowl. Add chicken pieces and mix well. Cover and set aside to marinate 30 minutes, turning chicken once or twice.

Heat oil in large skillet and sauté all peppers over medium heat 5 minutes.

Remove chicken from marinade, reserving liquid. Cut chicken into bite-size strips. Add chicken and half of marinade to skillet, and cook with peppers another 8 minutes. Add salt (or salt substitute) and pepper to taste.

Toast pita bread, then stuff each pocket with chicken mixture. Serve with Refreshing Dressing (see recipe below).

### Refreshing Dressing

1 cup plain non-fat yogurt
2 cloves garlic, minced
2 tablespoons fresh cilantro, minced
Salt, *or* salt substitute, and ground pepper
to taste

Combine all ingredients, and serve with chicken pitas.

### *Nutritional Data*

| PER SERVING | | EXCHANGES | |
|---|---|---|---|
| Calories: | 243 | Milk: | 0.4 |
| Fat (gm): | 7.9 | Vegetable: | 0.0 |
| Sat. fat (gm): | 1.2 | Fruit: | 0.0 |
| Cholesterol (mg): | 35.3 | Bread: | 1.1 |
| Sodium (mg): | 361 | Meat: | 1.5 |
| % Calories from fat: | 30 | Fat: | 1.3 |

# GRILLED TARRAGON CHICKEN

**Serves 4**

1 tablespoon fresh tarragon, finely chopped, *or*
  1½ teaspoons dried
1 tablespoon fresh parsley, chopped
  Salt, *or* salt substitute, and ground pepper
  to taste
1 tablespoon canola oil
4 boneless chicken breast halves, skin removed

C ombine tarragon, parsley, salt (or salt substitute), and pepper
and mix well. Brush chicken breasts lightly with canola oil, sprinkle with herb mixture, and place on grill or under broiler. Cook 5-6 minutes per side or until chicken is cooked through.

### Nutritional Data

| PER SERVING | | EXCHANGES | |
|---|---|---|---|
| Calories: | 189 | Milk: | 0.0 |
| Fat (gm): | 8.3 | Vegetable: | 0.0 |
| Sat. fat (gm): | 1.3 | Fruit: | 0.0 |
| Cholesterol (mg): | 68.4 | Bread: | 0.0 |
| Sodium (mg): | 77 | Meat: | 0.3 |
| % Calories from fat: | 21 | Fat: | 1.3 |

# POLLO MAGNIFICO

### Serves 4

1½ lbs. chicken pieces, skin removed
2 tablespoons diet margarine
¼ cup chunky salsa
¼ cup hickory- or mesquite-flavored barbecue
   sauce
⅛ cup water (optional)

**B** rown chicken in diet margarine. Combine salsa, barbecue sauce, and water (if necessary). Pour sauce over chicken and simmer, covered, 30-40 minutes until chicken is cooked through. Baste occasionally. Remove cover for last 10 minutes of cooking.

### Nutritional Data

| PER SERVING | | EXCHANGES | |
|---|---|---|---|
| Calories: | 260 | Milk: | 0.0 |
| Fat (gm): | 6.2 | Vegetable: | 0.4 |
| Sat. fat (gm): | 1.7 | Fruit: | 0.0 |
| Cholesterol (mg): | 100 | Bread: | 0.0 |
| Sodium (mg): | 386 | Meat: | 4.9 |
| % Calories from fat: | 22 | Fat: | 1.2 |

# CHICKEN IN A SNAP

**Serves 4**

4  boneless chicken breast halves, skin removed
½  cup non-fat sour cream, *or* plain non-fat yogurt
1  cup oyster crackers, crushed
¼  cup diet margarine, melted

**P**reheat oven to 375 degrees. Brush both sides of chicken with sour cream. Roll in crackers to coat. Place chicken on cookie sheet, and drizzle diet margarine over top. Bake 45 minutes.

### Nutritional Data

| PER SERVING | | EXCHANGES | |
|---|---|---|---|
| Calories: | 159 | Milk: | 0.3 |
| Fat (gm): | 2.8 | Vegetable: | 0.0 |
| Sat. fat (gm): | 0.6 | Fruit: | 0.0 |
| Cholesterol (mg): | 34.2 | Bread: | 0.8 |
| Sodium (mg): | 286 | Meat: | 1.5 |
| % Calories from fat: | 16 | Fat: | 0.2 |

# CHICKEN CHILI

*Serves 4*

½ lb. skinless chicken, ground
½ medium onion, chopped
1 small clove garlic, minced
1 16-oz. can stewed tomatoes, with juice
¼ teaspoon ground cumin
1 teaspoon chili powder
1 15½-oz. can kidney beans, drained, rinsed

C ombine meat, onion, and garlic in 2-quart, microwave-safe casserole and cover with paper towel. Microwave 3-4 minutes at High until chicken is cooked through. Stir and break up meat halfway through cooking. Drain liquid from dish.

Add remaining ingredients and mix well. Cover with casserole lid, and microwave 14-18 minutes at Medium, stirring halfway through cooking.

## Nutritional Data

| PER SERVING | | EXCHANGES | |
|---|---|---|---|
| Calories: | 182 | Milk: | 0.0 |
| Fat (gm): | 1.2 | Vegetable: | 1.3 |
| Sat. fat (gm): | 0.3 | Fruit: | 0.0 |
| Cholesterol (mg): | 32.9 | Bread: | 1.1 |
| Sodium (mg): | 417 | Meat: | 1.4 |
| % Calories from fat: | 6 | Fat: | 0.0 |

# SKINNY CHICKEN LO MEIN

### Serves 4

3½ ozs. rice noodles, uncooked
3 teaspoons sesame oil, divided
2 garlic cloves, minced
½ tablespoon fresh ginger, minced
½ teaspoon red pepper flakes
½ cup fresh basil, chopped
2 tablespoons dry sherry
2 tablespoons oyster sauce
¾ lb. cooked boneless chicken, skin removed, meat shredded

S oak rice noodles in warm water 10 minutes and drain.

In large skillet (or wok), heat 1 teaspoon sesame oil, and sauté garlic, ginger, and pepper flakes over high heat 1 minute.

Add rice noodles, basil, and sherry and stir-fry 1 minute more. Add remaining 2 teaspoons sesame oil and oyster sauce; stir-fry 1 minute more. Add chicken and stir-fry 1 minute more.

### Nutritional Data

| PER SERVING | | EXCHANGES | |
|---|---|---|---|
| Calories: | 184 | Milk: | 0.0 |
| Fat (gm): | 8.2 | Vegetable: | 0.0 |
| Sat. fat (gm): | 1.3 | Fruit: | 0.1 |
| Cholesterol (mg): | 49.3 | Bread: | 0.2 |
| Sodium (mg): | 139 | Meat: | 2.2 |
| % Calories from fat: | 31 | Fat: | 1.4 |

# ASIAN CHICKEN STIR-FRY

### *Serves 2*

1 cup cooked boneless chicken, skin removed, meat shredded
½ tablespoon low-sodium soy sauce
½ tablespoon dry sherry
½ teaspoon cornstarch
½ tablespoon water
2 tablespoons dried mushrooms
2 egg whites
½ tablespoon sesame oil
1 garlic clove, minced
1 slice fresh ginger, minced
4 ozs. canned bamboo shoots, sliced and drained
⅛ cup defatted chicken stock
½ tablespoon hoisin sauce
2 green onions, minced

C ombine chicken, soy sauce, sherry, cornstarch and water in bowl, and set aside 30 minutes. Soak dried mushrooms in warm water 20 minutes.

Cook egg whites in skillet 1 minute or in microwave 1 minute on High. Shred and set aside.

Heat oil in skillet (or wok) and stir-fry garlic and ginger 1 minute. Add chicken mixture, bamboo shoots, and mushrooms. Stir-fry over high heat 2 minutes. Add stock, egg whites, hoisin sauce, and green onions and stir-fry another 2 minutes.

### *Nutritional Data*

| PER SERVING | | EXCHANGES | |
|---|---|---|---|
| Calories: | 200 | Milk: | 0.0 |
| Fat (gm): | 5.2 | Vegetable: | 0.9 |
| Sat. fat (gm): | 1 | Fruit: | 0.0 |
| Cholesterol (mg): | 65.7 | Bread: | 0.0 |
| Sodium (mg): | 384 | Meat: | 3.4 |
| % Calories from fat: | 24 | Fat: | 0.7 |

# MICROWAVE CHICKEN SENSATION

*Serves 4*

   4 boneless chicken breast halves, skin removed
 ³⁄₄ cup water
   1 small onion, sliced
 ³⁄₄ teaspoon salt
 ¹⁄₈ teaspoon ground black pepper
 ¹⁄₂ bay leaf
 ¹⁄₈ lb. mushrooms, sliced
1¹⁄₂ tablespoons diet margarine
 ¹⁄₈ cup flour
   1 teaspoon dried parsley
 ¹⁄₂ teaspoon paprika
 ¹⁄₄ teaspoon ground cumin
 ¹⁄₄ cup skim milk

I n 1¹⁄₂-quart, microwave-safe baking dish, mix water, onion, salt, pepper, and bay leaf. Add chicken, placing thicker parts toward outside of dish. Cover and microwave on Medium-High 5 minutes, turning chicken once during cooking.

Remove chicken to warm bowl. Remove and discard bay leaf, and skim off any fat. Add mushrooms, and microwave on High 2 minutes. Remove liquid and vegetables and reserve.

In same baking dish, microwave diet margarine on High 30 seconds. Stir in flour, parsley, paprika, and cumin until smooth. Return vegetables and liquid to dish and stir in milk.

Cover and microwave on High 8 minutes or until thickened, stirring during cooking. Return chicken to baking dish, spoon gravy over chicken, cover, and microwave on Medium-High to heat thoroughly, about 3 minutes.

---

*Nutritional Data*

| PER SERVING | | EXCHANGES | |
|---|---|---|---|
| Calories: | 111 | Milk: | 0.1 |
| Fat (gm): | 5.1 | Vegetable: | 0.1 |
| Sat. fat (gm): | 0.9 | Fruit: | 0.0 |
| Cholesterol (mg): | 34.5 | Bread: | 0.0 |
| Sodium (mg): | 86 | Meat: | 1.5 |
| % Calories from fat: | 22 | Fat: | 0.9 |

# SUMPTUOUS MICRO CHICKEN BREASTS

*Serves 4*

2 egg whites
1 teaspoon canola oil
2 teaspoons skim milk
1 tablespoon Parmesan cheese, grated
3/4 cup seasoned breadcrumbs
4 chicken breast halves, skin removed
Fresh parsley

C ombine egg whites, oil, and milk in medium bowl. Combine cheese and breadcrumbs in plastic bag. Dip chicken pieces in egg mixture, coating evenly, then shake with crumb mixture.

Arrange chicken in shallow, microwave-safe casserole, with thicker pieces toward outside. Microwave 4 minutes at High. Rearrange chicken, and microwave 12-16 minutes at Medium-High until cooked through. Let stand 5 minutes. Garnish with parsley and serve.

## Nutritional Data

| PER SERVING | | EXCHANGES | |
|---|---|---|---|
| Calories: | 126 | Milk: | 0.0 |
| Fat (gm): | 2.5 | Vegetable: | 0.0 |
| Sat. fat (gm): | 0.5 | Fruit: | 0.0 |
| Cholesterol (mg): | 17.1 | Bread: | 0.9 |
| Sodium (mg): | 310 | Meat: | 0.1 |
| % Calories from fat: | 19 | Fat: | 0.3 |

# MICRO CHICKEN CHARDONNAY

### Serves 4

4 boneless chicken breast halves, skin removed
2 tablespoons diet margarine
1/2 teaspoon seasoned salt substitute
2 teaspoons lemon juice
2 tablespoons Chardonnay wine, *or* white grape juice
1/4 cup evaporated skim milk
1/2 teaspoon chicken bouillon granules
1 1/2 teaspoons cornstarch
Parsley

**P**ound chicken breasts flat with mallet and set aside.

Microwave diet margarine in microwave-safe casserole or baking dish 20-30 seconds on High until melted. Stir in lemon juice and seasoned salt. Roll chicken pieces in lemon mixture until well coated, then arrange with thickest portions to outside of dish.

Cover with waxed paper, and microwave 14 minutes at Medium, rearranging chicken halfway through. Drain remaining liquid from dish, and add water to make 1/4 cup.

In small bowl, combine reserved lemon mixture, wine, milk, bouillon, and cornstarch. Microwave 2-2 1/2 minutes on High until thickened. Pour over chicken. Garnish with parsley and serve.

### Nutritional Data

| PER SERVING | | EXCHANGES | |
|---|---|---|---|
| Calories: | 136 | Milk: | 0.1 |
| Fat (gm): | 6.5 | Vegetable: | 0.0 |
| Sat. fat (gm): | 1.2 | Fruit: | 0.0 |
| Cholesterol (mg): | 34.8 | Bread: | 0.1 |
| Sodium (mg): | 109 | Meat: | 1.5 |
| % Calories from fat: | 24 | Fat: | 1.2 |

# MICROWAVE "GRILLED" CHICKEN

*Serves 4*

4 chicken breast halves, skin removed
4 tablespoons lemon juice
4 tablespoons unflavored dry gelatin
4 teaspoons paprika
1 teaspoon garlic powder
1 teaspoon onion powder
1 teaspoon dry mustard
   Sweetener equivalent to 4 teaspoons sugar
2 teaspoons dried parsley

C oat chicken with lemon juice and set aside. Mix together remaining ingredients and sprinkle over chicken. Place chicken in 1-quart, microwave-safe casserole with thickest portions to outside of dish.

Cover with waxed paper. Microwave 3 minutes at High, then 12 minutes at Medium, rearranging chicken halfway through. Let stand 5 minutes before serving.

### Nutritional Data

| PER SERVING | | EXCHANGES | |
|---|---|---|---|
| Calories: | 141 | Milk: | 0.0 |
| Fat (gm): | 1.5 | Vegetable: | 0.0 |
| Sat. fat (gm): | 3.9 | Fruit: | 0.0 |
| Cholesterol (mg): | 68.4 | Bread: | 0.0 |
| Sodium (mg): | 84 | Meat: | 3.3 |
| % Calories from fat: | 10 | Fat: | 0.0 |

# RUSSIAN MICRO CHICKEN

**Serves 4**

- 4 boneless chicken breast halves, skin removed
- 4 teaspoons diet margarine
- 1 egg white
- 1 teaspoon canola oil
- 1½ teaspoons skim milk
- ½ cup seasoned breadcrumbs
- ½ teaspoon paprika
- 1 tablespoon caraway seeds

**P**ound chicken breasts flat with mallet, and place 1 teaspoon diet margarine on each piece. Roll up each breast and set aside.

Beat together egg white, oil, and milk. Dip chicken pieces in egg mixture, then roll in breadcrumbs. Sprinkle with paprika and caraway seeds.

Place in shallow, microwave-safe casserole, cover, and refrigerate 1 hour. Microwave, covered, 15-18 minutes at Medium-High or until cooked through, rearranging chicken halfway through cooking time. Let stand 5 minutes before serving.

### Nutritional Data

| PER SERVING | | EXCHANGES | |
|---|---|---|---|
| Calories: | 163 | Milk: | 0.0 |
| Fat (gm): | 6.4 | Vegetable: | 0.0 |
| Sat. fat (gm): | 1.1 | Fruit: | 0.0 |
| Cholesterol (mg): | 34.2 | Bread: | 0.6 |
| Sodium (mg): | 196 | Meat: | 1.6 |
| % Calories from fat: | 26 | Fat: | 1.0 |

# Micro Chicken Gone Crackers

*Serves 4*

1 egg white

¼ cup melted diet margarine

½ teaspoon salt, *or* salt substitute

1 cup SnackWell's Crackers (any flavor), crushed

2 lbs. boneless chicken pieces, skin removed

I n small bowl, whisk together egg white, diet margarine, and salt (or salt substitute) and set aside. Put cracker crumbs in plastic bag. Dip chicken pieces in egg mixture, then shake in bag with crumbs.

Place chicken pieces in microwave-safe dish with thickest portions to outside, and cover with waxed paper. Microwave at High 12-14 minutes, rearranging chicken halfway through cooking.

### Nutritional Data

| PER SERVING | | EXCHANGES | |
|---|---|---|---|
| Calories: | 310 | Milk: | 0.0 |
| Fat (gm): | 9.3 | Vegetable: | 0.0 |
| Sat. fat (gm): | 2 | Fruit: | 0.0 |
| Cholesterol (mg): | 88.4 | Bread: | 1.7 |
| Sodium (mg): | 799 | Meat: | 3.9 |
| % Calories from fat: | 26 | Fat: | 1.5 |

# MIRACLE MICRO STIR-FRY

### Serves 4

1 lb. boneless chicken breasts, skin removed,
cut into strips
2 teaspoons canola oil
1 cup broccoli, chopped
½ cup celery, sliced
½ cup mushrooms, sliced
½ cup (4 ozs.) bamboo shoots, sliced, drained
½ cup canned water chestnuts, sliced and
drained
2 teaspoons chicken bouillon granules dissolved
in ½ cup hot water
2 tablespoons white wine vinegar
1 tablespoon cornstarch
Sweetener equivalent to 3 teaspoons sugar

**P**lace chicken and oil in 2-quart, microwave-safe casserole. Cover and microwave 5-6 minutes at Medium-High until chicken is cooked through. Stir halfway through cooking. Remove chicken from casserole.

Combine broccoli, celery, mushrooms, bamboo shoots, and water chestnuts in casserole. Cover and microwave 5-6 minutes at High until vegetables are tender. Stir twice during cooking. Drain and reserve juices; set vegetables aside in casserole.

Combine bouillon mixture, vinegar, vegetable juices, cornstarch, and sweetener in glass measuring cup and mix until smooth. Cover and microwave 2-3 minutes at High until thickened. Add sauce and chicken to vegetables, cover, and microwave 2-3 minutes at High until heated through.

### Nutritional Data

| PER SERVING | | EXCHANGES | |
|---|---|---|---|
| Calories: | 174 | Milk: | 0.0 |
| Fat (gm): | 4 | Vegetable: | 0.7 |
| Sat. fat (gm): | 0.7 | Fruit: | 0.0 |
| Cholesterol (mg): | 65.9 | Bread: | 0.1 |
| Sodium (mg): | 361 | Meat: | 2.9 |
| % Calories from fat: | 21 | Fat: | 1.5 |

# MICRO REDUCED-CALORIE CHICKEN CASSEROLE

*Serves 4*

¼ cup celery, chopped

¼ cup onion, chopped

1 10-oz. package frozen mixed vegetables

½ can (half of 10½-oz. can) low-fat cream of mushroom soup

½ cup evaporated skim milk

2 cups cooked white rice

½ teaspoon seasoned salt substitute

1 cup cooked boneless chicken, skin removed, cubed

**C**ombine celery, onion, and mixed vegetables in 2-quart, microwave-safe casserole. Cover and microwave 5-7 minutes at High, until vegetables are tender.

Stir in remaining ingredients, cover, and microwave 3-4 minutes at High until heated through. Stir once halfway through cooking.

### Nutritional Data

| PER SERVING | | EXCHANGES | |
|---|---|---|---|
| Calories: | 276 | Milk: | 0.0 |
| Fat (gm): | 4 | Vegetable: | 1.6 |
| Sat. fat (gm): | 1.1 | Fruit: | 0.0 |
| Cholesterol (mg): | 10 | Bread: | 1.8 |
| Sodium (mg): | 97 | Meat: | 1.4 |
| % Calories from fat: | 30 | Fat: | 0.6 |

# 9.

# THE DRESSY CHICKEN
### *Fancier Fare*

◆

Appetizers, 105-109

◆

Main Dishes, 110-146

# PARISIAN CHICKEN TRIANGLES

**Serves 24** *(1 per person)*

4 ozs. boneless smoked chicken, skin removed
4 ozs. non-fat cream cheese
½ tablespoon Dijon mustard
1 tablespoon lemon juice
¼ teaspoon white pepper, finely ground
6 slices reduced-calorie white bread, crusts removed
1 tablespoon diet margarine, melted
4 radishes, sliced
Fresh dill

**P**reheat oven to 350 degrees. Using food processor and metal blade, process chicken 5-6 seconds. Add cream cheese, mustard, lemon juice, and pepper and process until smooth.

Brush bread slices with diet margarine. Cut each slice into 4 triangles and place, buttered side up, on baking sheet. Bake 12-15 minutes until toasted. Allow to cool.

Put chicken mixture into sealable plastic bag, snip one corner of bag, and apply 1 heaping teaspoon to each bread triangle. Garnish with radishes and dill.

### Nutritional Data

| PER SERVING | | EXCHANGES | |
|---|---|---|---|
| Calories: | 186 | Milk: | 0.0 |
| Fat (gm): | 1 | Vegetable: | 0.0 |
| Sat. fat (gm): | 0.6 | Fruit: | 0.0 |
| Cholesterol (mg): | 5.4 | Bread: | 0.2 |
| Sodium (mg): | 48 | Meat: | 0.2 |
| % Calories from fat: | 11 | Fat: | 0.3 |

# CHICKEN SPREAD FRANÇAISE

**Serves 8**

- 1 envelope unflavored gelatin
- 1½ cups water
- 1½ cups cooked boneless chicken, skin removed, meat cubed
- ¼ cup non-fat mayonnaise
- ⅛ teaspoon ground white pepper
- 2 tablespoons instant chicken bouillon granules
- ⅛ teaspoon garlic powder
- 1 teaspoon fresh dill weed
- ¼ cup onion, minced
  Non-stick cooking spray

 **S**prinkle gelatin over water in small saucepan. Heat over low heat until gelatin is completely dissolved.

In blender or food processor, combine gelatin with chicken, mayonnaise, pepper, chicken bouillon granules, garlic powder, and dill; process until smooth. Stir in onion and pour mixture into 3-cup mold coated with non-stick cooking spray. Chill overnight or until firm; unmold and serve.

### Nutritional Data

| PER SERVING | | EXCHANGES | |
|---|---|---|---|
| Calories: | 82 | Milk: | 0.0 |
| Fat (gm): | 1.6 | Vegetable: | 0.1 |
| Sat. fat (gm): | 0.5 | Fruit: | 0.1 |
| Cholesterol (mg): | 36.2 | Bread: | 0.0 |
| Sodium (mg): | 257 | Meat: | 1.3 |
| % Calories from fat: | 19 | Fat: | 0.0 |

# CHICKEN PÂTÉ DIJON

*Serves 20*

5-6 large spinach leaves, washed, trimmed
Non-stick cooking spray
1 lb. boneless chicken, skin removed, meat cubed
1 egg
1 egg white
2½ tablespoons olive oil
1 leek, trimmed and cleaned, white part only, chopped
1 tablespoon Dijon mustard
2 teaspoons capers, drained
1 teaspoon fresh garlic, minced
1 teaspoon white horseradish
1 teaspoon Worcestershire sauce
1 teaspoon fresh tarragon, minced
Salt, *or* salt substitute, and ground white pepper to taste
**Dijon Sauce** (see recipe below)

**P**reheat oven to 325 degrees.

Place spinach in large skillet over medium heat 1-2 minutes until leaves are wilted. Remove, drain, and set aside.

In blender or food processor, process remaining ingredients in batches until smooth. Place half of chicken mixture in 8-inch loaf pan coated with non-stick cooking spray. Press down slightly, and smooth with spoon or spatula. Add in layer, wilted spinach leaves, followed by remaining chicken.

Cover with aluminum foil, and set loaf pan in roasting pan containing 2 inches of hot water. Bake 1 hour. Remove from oven and allow to rest 15 minutes; then unmold pâté onto serving platter. Discard any excess liquid, cover, and chill at least 4 hours. Serve with Dijon Sauce (see recipe below).

*Dijon Sauce*

½ cup plain non-fat yogurt
1½ tablespoons non-fat mayonnaise
1 teaspoon Dijon mustard
1 tablespoon fresh chives, *or* scallions, chopped

Salt, *or* salt substitute, and ground white pepper to taste

Whisk together all ingredients. Spread over pâté and chill.

### *Nutritional Data*

| PER SERVING | | EXCHANGES | |
|---|---|---|---|
| Calories: | 48 | Milk: | 0.0 |
| Fat (gm): | 2.2 | Vegetable: | 0.0 |
| Sat. fat (gm): | 0.4 | Fruit: | 0.0 |
| Cholesterol (mg): | 19.7 | Bread: | 0.0 |
| Sodium (mg): | 50 | Meat: | 0.6 |
| % Calories from fat: | 32 | Fat: | 0.3 |

# GOLDEN HARVEST CURRIED "WINGLETS"

### Serves 20 *(1 per person)*

10 boneless chicken thighs, cut in half
4 tablespoons curry powder
4 tablespoons chutney, minced, divided
2 tablespoons lemon juice
¾ teaspoon salt
⅛ teaspoon cayenne
1 teaspoon low-sodium soy sauce
**Fresh Vegetable Sauce** (see recipe below)

**I** n large bowl, combine curry powder, 2 tablespoons chutney, lemon juice, salt, and cayenne, mixing well. Add chicken, stirring to coat. Cover and refrigerate at least 4 hours.

When ready to cook, preheat oven to 475 degrees. Combine soy sauce and remaining chutney in small bowl. Remove chicken from marinade, place on baking sheet, and bake 25 minutes.

Remove from oven, increase heat to broil, brush with soy sauce mixture, and place under broiler 1-2 minutes. Serve with Fresh Vegetable Sauce (see recipe below).

### Fresh Vegetable Sauce

1 cup plain non-fat yogurt
1 medium cucumber, seeded, minced
⅓ cup fresh coriander, minced
1 teaspoon lemon juice

Combine all ingredients and chill.

### Nutritional Data

| PER SERVING | | EXCHANGES | |
|---|---|---|---|
| Calories: | 113 | Milk: | 0.1 |
| Fat (gm): | 7.2 | Vegetable: | 0.1 |
| Sat. fat (gm): | 2 | Fruit: | 0.0 |
| Cholesterol (mg): | 40 | Bread: | 0.0 |
| Sodium (mg): | 59 | Meat: | 1.1 |
| % Calories from fat: | 14 | Fat: | 0.8 |

# ROASTED GARLIC CHICKEN

*Serves 11*

1 6-lb. roasting chicken
1 tablespoon olive oil
1¼ teaspoons dried sage, ground
  Salt, *or* salt substitute, and ground pepper to taste
2 whole garlic heads, separated into cloves
3 tablespoons dry white wine
2 tablespoons flour
¾ cup defatted chicken stock

**P**reheat oven to 450 degrees. Rinse chicken inside and out, pat dry, and rub inside and out with oil and sage. Use salt (or salt substitute) and pepper to taste.

Place chicken and garlic cloves in large roasting pan and bake 15 minutes. Remove garlic cloves from pan and reserve. Reduce oven to 375 degrees. Bake chicken another 1-1½ hours until cooked through. Remove chicken to serving platter, and drain all but 1 tablespoon of drippings from roasting pan.

Remove peels from garlic cloves, crush cloves in small bowl, and set aside.

On top of stove, add wine to roasting pan and bring to boil. Using whisk, slowly add flour and cook until mixture becomes a smooth paste, about 2 minutes. Add crushed garlic and cook another 2 minutes. Finish by slowly adding chicken stock.

Bring to boil, stirring constantly to dissolve any lumps. Cook 5-6 minutes until thickened. Serve chicken skinless with gravy on the side.

### Nutritional Data

| PER SERVING | | EXCHANGES | |
|---|---|---|---|
| Calories: | 300 | Milk: | 0.0 |
| Fat (gm): | 4 | Vegetable: | 0.0 |
| Sat. fat (gm): | 1 | Fruit: | 0.0 |
| Cholesterol (mg): | 100 | Bread: | 0.1 |
| Sodium (mg): | 212 | Meat: | 6.0 |
| % Calories from fat: | 14 | Fat: | 0.2 |

# MALABAR CHICKEN WITH YELLOW RICE

**Serves 4**

½ teaspoon canola oil

1 small onion, sliced

½ cup carrots, chopped

½ tablespoon fresh ginger, peeled and minced

½ tablespoon garlic, minced

¾ lb. boneless chicken pieces, skin removed, meat cut into strips

½ tablespoon curry powder

½ cup plain non-fat yogurt, room temperature

¼ cup almonds, sliced and toasted

¼ cup fresh cilantro

**Yellow Rice** (see recipe below)

 **P**repare Yellow Rice (see recipe below). Preheat oven to 350 degrees.

Heat oil in large skillet. Sauté onion over medium heat until brown, about 5 minutes. Increase heat and add carrots, ginger, and garlic; cook 1 minute. Add chicken and stir in curry powder.

Reduce heat, cover, and cook 5-6 minutes, stirring occasionally, until chicken is cooked through. Uncover and remove from heat. Stir in yogurt.

Pour half of Yellow Rice into baking dish. Spread chicken mixture over rice. Top with remaining rice, cover, and cook 25 minutes until heated through. Sprinkle with almonds and cilantro and serve.

*Yellow Rice*

1 teaspoon canola oil

1 teaspoon fresh ginger, peeled and minced

1 cup white basmati rice

1 tablespoon dried currants

1 tablespoon jalapeño pepper, chopped

½ teaspoon turmeric

3 whole cardamon pods

2 whole cloves

1 small cinnamon stick

Pinch saffron threads

1³/₄ cups water
³/₄ teaspoon salt, *or* salt substitute

Heat oil in saucepan over high heat, and sauté ginger for 30 seconds. Stir in rice, currants, jalapeño, turmeric, cardamon, cloves, cinnamon, and saffron and cook 1 minute. Add water and salt and bring to boil. Reduce heat, cover, and simmer 10-15 minutes until water is absorbed.

### Nutritional Data

| PER SERVING | | EXCHANGES | |
|---|---|---|---|
| Calories: | 363 | Milk: | 0.4 |
| Fat (gm): | 7.6 | Vegetable: | 0.2 |
| Sat. fat (gm): | 1.1 | Fruit: | 0.2 |
| Cholesterol (mg): | 49.9 | Bread: | 1.6 |
| Sodium (mg): | 189 | Meat: | 2.3 |
| % Calories from fat: | 19 | Fat: | 1.1 |

# SULTAN'S ROYAL CHICKEN

**Serves 4**

4  boneless chicken breast halves, skin removed
1  tablespoon lemon juice
1  green chili, minced
2  tablespoons fresh ginger, minced
3  cloves garlic, crushed
½  cup plain non-fat yogurt
1  teaspoon chili powder
   Non-stick cooking spray
1  tablespoon diet margarine
½  cup non-fat sour cream
   Salt, *or* salt substitute, to taste

**P**rick chicken breasts with fork, and rub well with lemon juice. In blender or food processor, combine green chili, ginger, garlic, yogurt, and chili powder and process until smooth. Combine with chicken in large bowl, stirring to coat; cover and refrigerate at least 3 hours.

Preheat oven to 425 degrees. Remove chicken from marinade and place in baking dish coated with non-stick spray. Reduce oven to 375 degrees, and bake chicken 45 minutes.

Melt diet margarine in large skillet, then add marinade and sour cream. Heat 4-5 minutes but do *not* boil. Lightly salt chicken, pour sauce over, and serve.

### Nutritional Data

| PER SERVING | | EXCHANGES | |
|---|---|---|---|
| Calories: | 125 | Milk: | 0.5 |
| Fat (gm): | 3.6 | Vegetable: | 0.0 |
| Sat. fat (gm): | 0.7 | Fruit: | 0.0 |
| Cholesterol (mg): | 34.8 | Bread: | 0.0 |
| Sodium (mg): | 108 | Meat: | 1.5 |
| % Calories from fat: | 28 | Fat: | 0.6 |

# THREE-CITRUS CHICKEN

### Serves 4

  2 tablespoons low-sodium soy sauce
  2 tablespoons dry sherry
  1 tablespoon cornstarch
  ¼ teaspoon ground white pepper
  1 lb. boneless chicken, skin removed, meat
     cubed
  ¼ cup defatted chicken stock
  3 tablespoons orange juice
  3 tablespoons lemon juice
  2 tablespoons lime juice
     Brown sugar substitute equivalent to 2 table-
     spoons brown sugar
  2 tablespoons canola oil
  1 teaspoon fresh ginger, minced
  1 teaspoon orange peel, grated
  1 teaspoon lemon peel, grated
  1 teaspoon lime peel, grated
  2 teaspoons cornstarch dissolved in 4 teaspoons
     water

**C**ombine first 4 ingredients and mix well. Add chicken and stir well to coat. Set aside for 30 minutes.

In separate bowl, mix together stock, juices, and brown sugar substitute. Remove chicken from marinade (discard marinade).

Heat oil and ginger in large skillet (or wok) over high heat 10-12 seconds. Add chicken and fruit peels, and stir-fry 2 minutes.

Add chicken stock mixture, reduce heat, and simmer 3-4 minutes until chicken is cooked through. Add cornstarch mixture, stirring constantly until sauce comes to boil and begins to thicken.

### Nutritional Data

| PER SERVING | | EXCHANGES | |
|---|---|---|---|
| Calories: | 214 | Milk: | 0.0 |
| Fat (gm): | 8.3 | Vegetable: | 0.0 |
| Sat. fat (gm): | 1.3 | Fruit: | 0.1 |
| Cholesterol (mg): | 65.7 | Bread: | 0.2 |
| Sodium (mg): | 528 | Meat: | 2.9 |
| % Calories from fat: | 26 | Fat: | 1.4 |

# MARIACHI CHICKEN MOLE

*Serves 4*

4 chicken breast halves, skin removed
2 tablespoons unsweetened cocoa powder
Sweetener equivalent to 3 tablespoons sugar
2 tablespoons water
Dash salt, *or* salt substitute
1 cup tomatoes, chopped
½ cup onion, chopped
2 cloves garlic, minced
2 fresh red chili peppers, seeded and chopped
2 fresh green chili peppers, seeded and chopped
¾ cup water
¼ cup sesame seeds, toasted
1 tablespoon raisins
¼ teaspoon ground cloves
¼ teaspoon ground cinnamon
⅛ teaspoon ground coriander
2 peppercorns
1 tablespoon canola oil

**B**roil chicken breasts 5-6 minutes per side until cooked through.
Combine cocoa, sweetener, water, and salt (or salt substitute) in small bowl, mixing well until dissolved, and set aside.

Using blender or food processor, combine tomatoes, onion, garlic, and both peppers; blend until smooth. Add water, sesame seeds, raisins, and spices and blend until pureed.

Heat oil in large skillet over medium heat, add tomato mixture, and cook 5 minutes, stirring constantly. Add chocolate mixture, and stir until heated through but do *not* boil.

Arrange chicken on serving platter, and spoon sauce over.

## *Nutritional Data*

| PER SERVING | | EXCHANGES | |
|---|---|---|---|
| Calories: | 150 | Milk: | 0.0 |
| Fat (gm): | 6.5 | Vegetable: | 0.6 |
| Sat. fat (gm): | 1.2 | Fruit: | 0.1 |
| Cholesterol (mg): | 34.2 | Bread: | 0.1 |
| Sodium (mg): | 50 | Meat: | 1.5 |
| % Calories from fat: | 27 | Fat: | 1.0 |

# TROPICAL MANGO CHICKEN SALAD

*Serves 4*

4 boneless chicken breast halves, skin removed
5 tablespoons olive oil, divided
2 green onions, minced
2 teaspoons fresh thyme leaves, divided
  Salt, *or* salt substitute, and ground pepper
  to taste
1 tablespoon balsamic vinegar
1 shallot, minced
4 cups romaine lettuce, shredded
1 small bunch watercress, stems discarded
½ cup red cabbage, shredded
1 large mango, peeled, pitted, and diced

**B** rush chicken with 1 tablespoon oil, then sprinkle with green onions, 1 teaspoon thyme, salt (or salt substitute), and pepper to taste. Set aside 30 minutes, turning once.

In small bowl, whisk together vinegar, shallot, and remaining thyme. Then whisk in remaining oil until dressing is emulsified.

Grill or broil chicken breasts 5-6 minutes per side until cooked through. Allow to cool and cut into cubes.

Combine romaine, watercress, cabbage, mango, and chicken, add vinaigrette dressing, and toss gently until coated.

### Nutritional Data

| PER SERVING | | EXCHANGES | |
|---|---|---|---|
| Calories: | 252 | Milk: | 0.0 |
| Fat (gm): | 17.8 | Vegetable: | 0.2 |
| Sat. fat (gm): | 2.5 | Fruit: | 0.5 |
| Cholesterol (mg): | 34.2 | Bread: | 0.0 |
| Sodium (mg): | 43 | Meat: | 1.5 |
| % Calories from fat: | 23 | Fat: | 3.3 |

# SINGAPORE LEMON CHICKEN

### Serves 4

¾ lb. chicken pieces, boneless, skin removed
1 tablespoon salt, *or* salt substitute
¼ teaspoon ground black pepper
¼ cup peanut oil, *or* canola oil
1 tablespoon onion, minced
1 clove garlic, minced
½ teaspoon ground coriander
¼ teaspoon ground cumin
¼ teaspoon red pepper flakes
¼ teaspoon turmeric
2 tablespoons low-sodium soy sauce
2 lemons, seeded and quartered
2 cups cooked white rice, *or* pasta

**S**prinkle chicken with salt (or salt substitute) and pepper. Heat oil in large skillet over medium heat, and brown chicken on all sides. Add onion and garlic, and sauté until golden.

Add coriander, cumin, red pepper flakes, and turmeric. Then add soy sauce, reduce heat, and cover pan. Cook on low heat 20-30 minutes until chicken is cooked through.

Squeeze 1 lemon on chicken before serving; garnish with remaining lemon quarters. Serve with rice or pasta.

### Nutritional Data

| PER SERVING | | EXCHANGES | |
|---|---|---|---|
| Calories: | 323 | Milk: | 0.0 |
| Fat (gm): | 14 | Vegetable: | 0.0 |
| Sat. fat (gm): | 1.1 | Fruit: | 0.0 |
| Cholesterol (mg): | 63 | Bread: | 1.3 |
| Sodium (mg): | 483 | Meat: | 2.7 |
| % Calories from fat: | 30 | Fat: | 2.7 |

# LIME-PECAN CHICKEN

**Serves 16**

1½ teaspoons cornstarch
½ cup cold water
3 boneless chicken breasts, skin removed, cut into strips
Salt, *or* salt substitute, and pepper to taste
2 tablespoons canola oil
1 cup defatted chicken stock
4 tablespoons lime juice, divided
3 teaspoons Dijon mustard
Brown sugar substitute equivalent to 1 tablespoon brown sugar
1½ tablespoons diet margarine, melted
⅓ cup vermouth
¾ lb. mushrooms, sliced
¼ cup large pimiento-stuffed olives
3 cups cooked rice
¼ cup pecans, chopped

**C**ombine cornstarch and water in bowl; stir until smooth.
Sprinkle chicken strips with salt (or salt substitute) and pepper.
In large skillet, heat oil over medium heat, and sauté chicken 8 minutes, turning once. Remove chicken from skillet.
Using same skillet, add stock, 3 tablespoons lime juice, mustard, and brown sugar substitute, stirring constantly. Add cornstarch mixture and cook 3 minutes, stirring constantly, until sauce thickens. Whisk in remaining lime juice and diet margarine.
Return chicken to skillet, add vermouth, and cover. Simmer about 5 minutes, then add mushrooms and olives. Simmer another 5 minutes until chicken is cooked through. Serve over cooked rice, and garnish with pecans.

---

**Nutritional Data**

| PER SERVING | | EXCHANGES | |
|---|---|---|---|
| Calories: | 215 | Milk: | 0.0 |
| Fat (gm): | 11 | Vegetable: | 0.0 |
| Sat. fat (gm): | 3.5 | Fruit: | 0.1 |
| Cholesterol (mg): | 16 | Bread: | 1.0 |
| Sodium (mg): | 211 | Meat: | 0.7 |
| % Calories from fat: | 30 | Fat: | 3.1 |

# ROAST CHICKEN AND HOLIDAY STUFFING

◆

### Serves 16

### Roast Chicken

1 8-lb. roasting chicken, *or* capon, giblets
   removed
   Dried sage

**P**reheat oven to 475 degrees. Rinse and pat dry chicken, then season lightly with sage. Place in roasting pan. If you also prepare Stuffing (see recipe below), lightly fill central cavity with mixture. Put in oven and reduce heat to 350 degrees.

Bake 20 minutes per pound, basting with own juices 2-3 times. Cover lightly with aluminum foil if chicken begins to get too brown. If using Stuffing, remove from chicken, and allow chicken to cool 15 minutes before carving.

Remove chicken skin and serve without Stuffing to attain nutritional quantities stated below. Low-calorie cranberry sauce or cranberry chutney also make ideal accompaniments.

To cook any remaining Stuffing that could not fit inside chicken, place in small casserole sprayed with non-stick cooking spray, cover, and bake in 350-degree oven 30-40 minutes.

◆

### Nutritional Data for Chicken

| PER SERVING | | EXCHANGES | |
|---|---|---|---|
| Calories: | 300 | Milk: | 0.0 |
| Fat (gm): | 7.2 | Vegetable: | 0.0 |
| Sat. fat (gm): | 2 | Fruit: | 0.0 |
| Cholesterol (mg): | 100 | Bread: | 0.0 |
| Sodium (mg): | 111 | Meat: | 4.6 |
| % Calories from fat: | 27 | Fat: | 0.0 |

### Holiday Stuffing

*Croutons*

2 lbs. reduced-calorie whole-grain bread, cubed
2 tablespoons olive oil
3 teaspoons dried thyme
1½ teaspoons sage
1½ teaspoons rosemary, crumbled
½ teaspoon paprika

Preheat oven to 350 degrees. Place all ingredients in large bowl and toss. Bake in single layer on baking sheet 25 minutes. Remove from oven, transfer to bowl, and set aside.

*Holiday Stuffing*

2 tablespoons olive oil
1 cup onion, chopped
½ cup celery, chopped
½ cup fresh fennel, chopped
1 lb. turkey sausage
2 tart apples, cored and cubed
½ cup dried cherries, *or* raisins
2 tablespoons orange peel, grated
1½ teaspoons dried thyme
1½ teaspoons sage
1½ teaspoons dried rosemary, crumbled
½ cup orange juice
½ cup defatted chicken stock
Salt, *or* salt substitute, and ground pepper
to taste

Heat oil in medium skillet, add onion, celery, and fennel, and cook over low heat 7-9 minutes. Remove vegetables with slotted spoon and add to Croutons.

Crumble turkey sausage into skillet, and brown over medium heat. Remove with slotted spoon and add to Croutons. Add remaining ingredients to Crouton mixture and allow to cool.

### Nutritional Data for Stuffing

| PER SERVING | | EXCHANGES | |
|---|---|---|---|
| Calories: | 277 | Milk: | 0.0 |
| Fat (gm): | 9.7 | Vegetable: | 0.3 |
| Sat. fat (gm): | 2.2 | Fruit: | 0.8 |
| Cholesterol (mg): | 29.2 | Bread: | 1.6 |
| Sodium (mg): | 623 | Meat: | 1.0 |
| % Calories from fat: | 29 | Fat: | 0.7 |

# ZUCCHINI-STUFFED CHICKEN BREASTS

***Serves 4***

4  boneless chicken breast halves, skin removed
2  tablespoons diet margarine
½  cup onion, chopped
2  cups mushrooms, chopped
1  cup zucchini, coarsely shredded
¼  teaspoon ground nutmeg
⅛  teaspoon garlic powder
3  tablespoons dry breadcrumbs
1  egg white
    Salt, *or* salt substitute, and ground pepper to
    taste
    Paprika
    Dried parsley

reheat oven to 350 degrees. Pound chicken breasts flat with mallet. Set aside.

Melt diet margarine in large skillet, and cook onions and mushrooms over medium heat 8-10 minutes until tender. Remove skillet from heat and add zucchini, nutmeg, garlic powder, breadcrumbs, egg white, salt (or salt substitute), and pepper. Mix well and divide evenly, placing ¼ of mixture in center of each chicken breast.

Fold edges of breast fillets, and place seam down in shallow pan. Sprinkle with paprika and parsley, cover, and bake 40 minutes.

***Nutritional Data***

| PER SERVING | | EXCHANGES | |
|---|---|---|---|
| Calories: | 126 | Milk: | 0.0 |
| Fat (gm): | 6.5 | Vegetable: | 0.0 |
| Sat. fat (gm): | 1.2 | Fruit: | 0.0 |
| Cholesterol (mg): | 34.2 | Bread: | 0.1 |
| Sodium (mg): | 118 | Meat: | 1.6 |
| % Calories from fat: | 28 | Fat: | 1.1 |

# Exotic Tomato Chicken

**Serves 4**

1/2 cup dry white wine
1 1-lb. can crushed tomatoes
1/4 cup low-sodium tomato paste
2 tablespoons instant chicken bouillon granules
1 bay leaf
1/4 teaspoon dried thyme
1/4 teaspoon ground black pepper
1 1/2 cups water
1 tablespoon canola oil
2 teaspoons lemon juice
1 cup onion, sliced
2 cloves garlic, minced
2 lbs. boneless chicken, skin removed
2 cups mushrooms, sliced

**C**ombine white wine, tomatoes with juice, tomato paste, chicken-flavored granules, bay leaf, thyme, pepper, and water in medium-size bowl. Mix well and set aside.

In large covered casserole, heat oil and lemon juice over medium heat, and sauté onion and garlic until browned. Add chicken and tomato mixture. Bring to boil, reduce heat, cover, and simmer 1 1/4 hours, stirring occasionally.

Add mushrooms and cook another 15 minutes. Remove and discard bay leaf before serving.

## Nutritional Data

| PER SERVING | | EXCHANGES | |
|---|---|---|---|
| Calories: | 125 | Milk: | 0.0 |
| Fat (gm): | 1.4 | Vegetable: | 1.5 |
| Sat. fat (gm): | 0.3 | Fruit: | 0.0 |
| Cholesterol (mg): | 34.4 | Bread: | 0.0 |
| Sodium (mg): | 343 | Meat: | 1.5 |
| % Calories from fat: | 10 | Fat: | 0.5 |

# BUDAPEST CHICKEN

**Serves 4**

- 1 tablespoon dry sherry
- ⅓ cup defatted chicken stock
- 1 medium onion, sliced
- 2 garlic cloves, minced
- ¼ lb. mushrooms, sliced
  Salt, *or* salt substitute, and ground pepper
  to taste
- 4 boneless chicken breast halves, skin removed
- ¾ cup plain non-fat yogurt
- ¼ cup non-fat sour cream
- 1½ tablespoons paprika

 reheat oven to 375 degrees. Combine sherry and stock in small bowl and set aside.

In large skillet, cook onion, garlic, and mushrooms over low heat in 2 tablespoons of sherry mixture. Add salt (or salt substitute) and pepper to taste, remove vegetables from skillet, and set aside.

Pound chicken breasts flat with mallet. In separate bowl, combine yogurt, sour cream, and paprika.

Heat 2 tablespoons of sherry mixture in large skillet, add chicken, and cook over medium heat 2 minutes. Turn chicken over, add remaining sherry mixture, cook another 2-3 minutes, and reduce heat.

Remove 1 tablespoon sherry mixture from skillet, stir into yogurt mixture, and pour yogurt over chicken. Heat 1 minute, then stir in mushrooms and onions, and cook 1 minute more before serving.

### Nutritional Data

| PER SERVING | | EXCHANGES | |
|---|---|---|---|
| Calories: | 105 | Milk: | 0.4 |
| Fat (gm): | 0.9 | Vegetable: | 0.5 |
| Sat. fat (gm): | 0.3 | Fruit: | 0.0 |
| Cholesterol (mg): | 35 | Bread: | 0.0 |
| Sodium (mg): | 148 | Meat: | 1.5 |
| % Calories from fat: | 8 | Fat: | 0.1 |

# Pasta Primavera con Pollo

### Serves 4

- 1 cup broccoli florets,
- 1 cup carrots, peeled, thinly sliced
- 1 cup cauliflower, sliced
- 1½ lbs. boneless chicken, skin removed, meat cut into strips
- 2 shallots, minced
- 1 tablespoon dry white wine
- ½ teaspoon ground white pepper
- 1 teaspoon diet margarine
- 2 teaspoons flour
- 1¼ cups skim milk
- 2 tablespoons Parmesan cheese, grated
- 1 teaspoon dried basil
- ⅛ teaspoon salt, *or* salt substitute
- 3 ozs. fettucine noodles, cooked and drained

**S**team vegetables 3-4 minutes and set aside.

Place chicken, shallots, and wine in large skillet, bring to boil, reduce heat, and simmer 5-6 minutes until chicken is cooked through. Remove chicken and sprinkle pieces with pepper.

Discard liquid, then melt diet margarine in same saucepan. Add flour and cook 2 minutes on medium heat, stirring constantly. Reduce heat and whisk in milk a little at a time until mixture is smooth. Stir in cheese until it melts, then add basil and salt.

Fold in chicken pieces and vegetables, cooking 1 minute. Add noodles and cook 1 more minute until heated through, but do *not* bring to boil. Transfer to serving bowl and serve.

### Nutritional Data

| PER SERVING | | EXCHANGES | |
|---|---|---|---|
| Calories: | 273 | Milk: | 0.3 |
| Fat (gm): | 4.3 | Vegetable: | 1.0 |
| Sat. fat (gm): | 1.4 | Fruit: | 0.0 |
| Cholesterol (mg): | 102 | Bread: | 0.1 |
| Sodium (mg): | 243 | Meat: | 4.5 |
| % Calories from fat: | 15 | Fat: | 0.3 |

# DELHI CHICKEN

**Serves 4**

2  garlic cloves, minced
½  tablespoon ground coriander
1  teaspoon ground cumin
8  ozs. non-fat yogurt
1  tablespoon fresh ginger, minced
1  tablespoon lime juice
½  teaspoon cayenne pepper
1  teaspoon turmeric
2  tablespoons fresh coriander, chopped
½  teaspoon salt, *or* salt substitute
4  boneless chicken breast halves, skin removed

C ombine all ingredients except chicken in large bowl and mix well. Add chicken breasts, coating with sauce; cover and refrigerate 24 hours. Remove chicken and discard marinade. Grill or broil chicken breasts 5-6 minutes per side until cooked through.

### Nutritional Data

| PER SERVING | | EXCHANGES | |
|---|---|---|---|
| Calories: | 96 | Milk: | 0.4 |
| Fat (gm): | 0.8 | Vegetable: | 0.0 |
| Sat. fat (gm): | 0.3 | Fruit: | 0.0 |
| Cholesterol (mg): | 35.2 | Bread: | 0.0 |
| Sodium (mg): | 82 | Meat: | 1.5 |
| % Calories from fat: | 8 | Fat: | 0.0 |

# ELEGANT CHICKEN AND LEEKS

### Serves 4

1 8-oz. can low-sodium tomato sauce
2 garlic cloves
1 teaspoon fresh mint, chopped
½ teaspoon fresh ginger, chopped
¼ teaspoon cinnamon
  Sweetener equivalent to ½ teaspoon sugar
½ teaspoon low-sodium soy sauce
½ teaspoon chili powder
4 boneless chicken breast halves, skin removed
1 leek, trimmed and cleaned, white portion only, sliced
2 tablespoons water
½ tablespoon diet margarine
⅛ teaspoon salt, or salt substitute

ombine first 8 ingredients in blender or food processor and blend until smooth.

Pound chicken breasts flat with mallet. Pour tomato mixture over breasts, cover, and refrigerate at least 2 hours.

In small skillet, cook leeks with 2 tablespoons water over medium heat 4-5 minutes. Add diet margarine and salt, and stir until leeks are well coated. Cover and set aside.

Grill or broil chicken breasts 5-6 minutes per side until cooked through. Serve with warm leeks.

### Nutritional Data

| PER SERVING | | EXCHANGES | |
|---|---|---|---|
| Calories: | 92.3 | Milk: | 0.0 |
| Fat (gm): | 2.2 | Vegetable: | 0.7 |
| Sat. fat (gm): | 0.5 | Fruit: | 0.0 |
| Cholesterol (mg): | 34.2 | Bread: | 0.0 |
| Sodium (mg): | 94 | Meat: | 1.5 |
| % Calories from fat: | 22 | Fat: | 0.3 |

# GRAN PARADISO CHICKEN BREASTS

### Serves 4

- 4 boneless chicken breast halves, skin removed
- ½ cup breadcrumbs made from stale reduced-calorie bread
- 1½ tablespoons fresh thyme, chopped
- ½ teaspoon paprika
- ½ teaspoon ground black pepper
- 2½ ozs. low-fat mozzarella cheese, coarsely chopped
- 1 bunch fresh basil
  Non-stick cooking spray

reheat oven to 375 degrees. Pound chicken breasts flat with mallet.

In large bowl, combine breadcrumbs, thyme, paprika, and pepper. Dip each chicken piece in crumb mixture to coat well. Place ¼ of cheese and basil in center of each chicken breast.

Fold edges and place, seam down, in shallow pan coated with non-stick cooking spray. Bake 20 minutes.

### Nutritional Data

| PER SERVING | | EXCHANGES | |
|---|---|---|---|
| Calories: | 154 | Milk: | 0.0 |
| Fat (gm): | 4.1 | Vegetable: | 0.0 |
| Sat. fat (gm): | 2.1 | Fruit: | 0.0 |
| Cholesterol (mg): | 31 | Bread: | 0.9 |
| Sodium (mg): | 545 | Meat: | 2.2 |
| % Calories from fat: | 30 | Fat: | 0.3 |

# BALTIC CHICKEN WITH APRICOTS

### Serves 4

- 1 teaspoon salt, *or* salt substitute
- 1/4 teaspoon dried thyme
- 1/4 teaspoon dried rosemary, crumbled
- 1/4 teaspoon dried oregano
- 4 boneless chicken breast halves, skin removed
  Non-stick cooking spray
- 1 16-oz. can apricots in light syrup
- 2 tablespoons flour
- 1 tablespoon diet margarine
- 2 tablespoons dry white wine
- 1³/4 cups defatted chicken stock

**P**reheat oven to 375 degrees. Mix together salt (or salt substitute), thyme, rosemary, and oregano and rub over all sides of chicken breasts. Place chicken in baking pan coated with non-stick cooking spray, and bake 40-45 minutes until cooked through.

Drain apricots and reserve 1/4 cup of juice.

In large skillet, cook flour over medium heat 2 minutes, stirring constantly. Add diet margarine and stir until melted. Add reserved apricot juice, wine, and stock to skillet, stirring until thickened. Add apricots and then chicken, spooning sauce and fruit over chicken breasts. Simmer 3 minutes and serve.

### Nutritional Data

| PER SERVING | | EXCHANGES | |
|---|---|---|---|
| Calories: | 183 | Milk: | 0.0 |
| Fat (gm): | 1.6 | Vegetable: | 0.0 |
| Sat. fat (gm): | 0.4 | Fruit: | 1.4 |
| Cholesterol (mg): | 34.2 | Bread: | 0.2 |
| Sodium (mg): | 381 | Meat: | 1.5 |
| % Calories from fat: | 8 | Fat: | 0.1 |

# Chicken Breasts with Vegetable Stuffing

**Serves 4**

- 8 Rye Krisps, crushed
- ½ cup onion, minced
- ¼ cup celery, minced
- 2 cups mushrooms, chopped
- ¼ cup water
- ¼ teaspoon sage
- ¼ teaspoon ground thyme
- ¼ teaspoon poultry seasoning
  Salt, *or* salt substitute, and ground pepper
  to taste
- 4 boneless chicken breast halves, skin removed
- ⅛ teaspoon paprika

P reheat oven to 350 degrees. Mix together all ingredients except chicken and paprika. Add more water if mixture seems dry.

Pound chicken breasts flat with mallet. Place ¼ of stuffing in center of each chicken piece. Fold edges and place seam down in shallow pan. Sprinkle with paprika, and bake 30-40 minutes until chicken is cooked through.

---

### Nutritional Data

| PER SERVING | | EXCHANGES | |
|---|---|---|---|
| Calories: | 148 | Milk: | 0.0 |
| Fat (gm): | 1.7 | Vegetable: | 1.1 |
| Sat. fat (gm): | 0.3 | Fruit: | 0.0 |
| Cholesterol (mg): | 34.2 | Bread: | 0.7 |
| Sodium (mg): | 170 | Meat: | 1.5 |
| % Calories from fat: | 10 | Fat: | 0.0 |

# MUSHROOM CHICKEN DELIGHT

### Serves 4

4 boneless chicken breast halves, skin removed
Non-stick cooking spray
Salt, *or* salt substitute, and ground pepper to taste
1 teaspoon celery seed
½ teaspoon dried marjoram
4 tablespoons lemon juice
3 cups mushrooms, sliced

P reheat oven to 350 degrees. Place chicken in baking pan coated with non-stick cooking spray. Sprinkle with salt (or salt substitute), pepper, celery seed, and marjoram.

Add lemon juice to pan, then spread mushrooms over chicken. Cover and bake 30 minutes. Reduce temperature to 325 degrees, remove cover, and bake another 15 minutes or until chicken is cooked through.

### Nutritional Data

| PER SERVING | | EXCHANGES | |
|---|---|---|---|
| Calories: | 109 | Milk: | 0.0 |
| Fat (gm): | 1.6 | Vegetable: | 1.6 |
| Sat. fat (gm): | 0.3 | Fruit: | 0.0 |
| Cholesterol (mg): | 34.2 | Bread: | 0.0 |
| Sodium (mg): | 46 | Meat: | 1.5 |
| % Calories from fat: | 12 | Fat: | 0.0 |

# CHICKEN ROMA

*Serves 4*

- 4 boneless chicken breast halves, skin removed
- ⅓ cup flour
- 2 tablespoons diet margarine, melted
- ¼ cup grated Romano cheese
- ½ cup dry white wine

**P** reheat oven to 350 degrees. Coat chicken pieces with flour and place in baking dish. Brush with melted diet margarine. Bake 30 minutes, basting once. Sprinkle with grated cheese and add wine. Bake another 30 minutes, basting once.

## Nutritional Data

| PER SERVING | | EXCHANGES | |
|---|---|---|---|
| Calories: | 197 | Milk: | 0.0 |
| Fat (gm): | 8.2 | Vegetable: | 0.0 |
| Sat. fat (gm): | 2.2 | Fruit: | 0.0 |
| Cholesterol (mg): | 40.7 | Bread: | 0.5 |
| Sodium (mg): | 167 | Meat: | 1.8 |
| % Calories from fat: | 28 | Fat: | 1.8 |

# CHICKEN PHYLLO SUPREME

### Serves 6

- 2 cups broccoli florets
- 2 cups cooked boneless chicken, skin removed, meat cubed
- 1½ cups non-fat sour cream
- ¼ cup Parmesan cheese, grated
- 8 sheets phyllo
- 2 tablespoons diet margarine, melted

reheat oven to 375 degrees. Steam broccoli 4-5 minutes, drain, and rinse with cool water. Set aside.

Combine chicken with sour cream, add broccoli and Parmesan cheese, and set aside.

Lay out one sheet of phyllo and brush lightly with melted diet margarine. Repeat until you have 4 layers of phyllo. Place ½ of chicken mixture on phyllo, leaving 2-inch border. Starting at small end, roll up, jellyroll style. Place on baking sheet. Repeat process with remaining phyllo and chicken.

Bake 20-25 minutes until golden. Allow to cool slightly, and slice each roll into 4 pieces before serving.

### Nutritional Data

| PER SERVING | | EXCHANGES | |
|---|---|---|---|
| Calories: | 277 | Milk: | 0.5 |
| Fat (gm): | 31.5 | Vegetable: | 0.3 |
| Sat. fat (gm): | 2.4 | Fruit: | 0.0 |
| Cholesterol (mg): | 67.5 | Bread: | 0.6 |
| Sodium (mg): | 308 | Meat: | 2.4 |
| % Calories from fat: | 29 | Fat: | 1.1 |

# CHICKEN AND PENNE FROM HEAVEN

***Serves 4***

1½ teaspoons olive oil
1 large onion, minced
1 clove garlic, crushed
1 28-oz. can Italian peeled tomatoes with juice
¼ teaspoon red pepper flakes, crushed
10 ozs. penne pasta, cooked as directed on
    package
2 cups cooked boneless chicken, skin removed,
    meat cubed
3 ozs. low-fat mozzarella cheese, diced
1 tablespoon parsley, chopped
2 tablespoons Parmesan cheese, grated

I n large skillet, heat olive oil and sauté onion and garlic over
medium heat 5 minutes, stirring occasionally. Add tomatoes with
juice and pepper flakes, and continue cooking 15-20 minutes until sauce
thickens.

Combine pasta and chicken in large serving bowl, pour tomato sauce
over, and toss well. Add mozzarella and parsley and toss again. Sprinkle
with Parmesan cheese and serve.

***Nutritional Data***

| PER SERVING | | EXCHANGES | |
|---|---|---|---|
| Calories: | 367 | Milk: | 0.0 |
| Fat (gm): | 8.7 | Vegetable: | 2.2 |
| Sat. fat (gm): | 3.7 | Fruit: | 0.0 |
| Cholesterol (mg): | 79.7 | Bread: | 1.3 |
| Sodium (mg): | 271 | Meat: | 3.9 |
| % Calories from fat: | 21 | Fat: | 0.7 |

# TANTE BELLA'S STUFFED CABBAGE

**Serves 4**

1 small head cabbage
1 tablespoon canola oil
½ cup onion, chopped
1 clove garlic, minced
½ lb. skinless chicken, ground
½ cup white rice, cooked
½ cup raisins
2 egg whites
2 teaspoons caraway seeds
¾ teaspoon salt, *or* salt substitute
½ teaspoon ground black pepper
1 8-oz. can tomato puree
Brown sugar substitute equivalent to 2 tablespoons brown sugar
2 tablespoons cider vinegar

reheat oven to 350 degrees. Core cabbage, finely chop core, and set aside.

Bring large pot of water to boil. Place whole cored cabbage in boiling water, and cook 10-12 minutes until leaves are tender but not mushy. Drain and rinse cabbage and set aside.

In skillet, heat oil and sauté onion and garlic 5 minutes. Add chicken and chopped cabbage core, and cook another 5-6 minutes until cooked through. Combine chicken mixture, rice, raisins, egg whites, caraway seeds, salt (or salt substitute), and pepper in large bowl and mix well.

Carefully separate cabbage leaves, and cut away thick central ribs. Place ¼ of chicken mixture in each leaf, roll up, and tuck in sides. Secure with toothpick, and place rolls in large baking dish.

In small bowl, combine tomato puree, brown sugar substitute, and cider vinegar and mix well. Pour over stuffed cabbage. Cover dish and bake 40-45 minutes.

## *Nutritional Data*

| PER SERVING | | EXCHANGES | |
|---|---|---|---|
| Calories: | 235 | Milk: | 0.0 |
| Fat (gm): | 4.8 | Vegetable: | 1.7 |
| Sat. fat (gm): | 0.7 | Fruit: | 1.2 |
| Cholesterol (mg): | 32.9 | Bread: | 0.4 |
| Sodium (mg): | 92 | Meat: | 1.7 |
| % Calories from fat: | 18 | Fat: | 0.7 |

# Coq au Vin Marseille

*Serves 4*

4 boneless chicken breast halves, skin removed
1 teaspoon salt, *or* salt substitute
 Ground black pepper to taste
1 teaspoon garlic powder
¼ lb. fresh button mushrooms, sliced
3 tablespoons fresh tarragon, chopped
¾ cup dry white wine

**P**lace chicken breasts on baking sheet, and sprinkle with salt (or salt substitute), pepper, and garlic powder. Broil 1-2 minutes per side until slightly browned.

Remove chicken from broiler, and reduce oven heat to 350 degrees. Place chicken in baking dish, sprinkle with mushrooms, tarragon, and wine. Cover and bake 1 hour, basting 2-3 times.

### Nutritional Data

| PER SERVING | | EXCHANGES | |
|---|---|---|---|
| Calories: | 101 | Milk: | 0.0 |
| Fat (gm): | 0.9 | Vegetable: | 0.2 |
| Sat. fat (gm): | 0.2 | Fruit: | 0.0 |
| Cholesterol (mg): | 34.2 | Bread: | 0.0 |
| Sodium (mg): | 41 | Meat: | 1.5 |
| % Calories from fat: | 22 | Fat: | 0.6 |

# CHICKEN RIVIERA

**Serves 4**

4 boneless chicken breast halves, skin removed
½ cup low-fat Swiss cheese, shredded
¼ cup lean cooked ham, minced
2 teaspoons Dijon mustard
¼ cup flour
¼ teaspoon salt
1 egg
2 tablespoons water
⅓ cup dry plain breadcrumbs
2 tablespoons canola oil

**P**ound chicken breasts flat with mallet and set aside. Combine cheese and ham in small bowl. Brush top of chicken with mustard, and place ¼ of cheese and ham mixture on center of each chicken piece. Fold over ends and roll up each piece, jellyroll style, pressing seams to seal. Cover and refrigerate at least 1 hour.

Mix flour and salt in one dish, egg and water in another, and place breadcrumbs in a third. Dip chicken rolls first in flour, then in egg, and finally in breadcrumbs. Cover and refrigerate another 1 hour. Preheat oven to 350 degrees.

Heat oil in skillet and brown chicken rolls 1-2 minutes per side over medium heat until golden brown. Transfer to baking dish, and bake 25-30 minutes until chicken is cooked through.

### Nutritional Data

| PER SERVING | | EXCHANGES | |
|---|---|---|---|
| Calories: | 245 | Milk: | 0.0 |
| Fat (gm): | 10.4 | Vegetable: | 0.0 |
| Sat. fat (gm): | 2.2 | Fruit: | 0.0 |
| Cholesterol (mg): | 78.8 | Bread: | 0.8 |
| Sodium (mg): | 498 | Meat: | 2.5 |
| % Calories from fat: | 29 | Fat: | 1.4 |

# ITALIAN BREADED CHICKEN

### Serves 4

4 boneless chicken breast halves, skin removed
¼ cup flour
1 cup dry, Italian-style, seasoned breadcrumbs
¼ teaspoon salt
2 eggs, beaten
2 tablespoons canola oil

P ound chicken breasts flat with mallet, dip in flour to coat both sides, and set aside. Combine breadcrumbs and salt in small bowl. Dip chicken pieces in egg, then roll in breadcrumbs until coated.

Heat oil in large skillet, and sauté chicken 3-4 minutes per side over medium heat until golden brown and cooked through.

### Nutritional Data

| PER SERVING | | EXCHANGES | |
|---|---|---|---|
| Calories: | 262 | Milk: | 0.0 |
| Fat (gm): | 11.6 | Vegetable: | 0.0 |
| Sat. fat (gm): | 3 | Fruit: | 0.0 |
| Cholesterol (mg): | 100 | Bread: | 1.0 |
| Sodium (mg): | 698 | Meat: | 2.3 |
| % Calories from fat: | 30 | Fat: | 1.7 |

# CARIBBEAN CHICKEN AND BLACK BEANS

---

### Serves 4

1¾ cups defatted chicken stock
½ cup coconut
1 tablespoon diet margarine
1 cup uncooked white rice
1 15-oz. can black beans, drained and rinsed
½ cup green onion, sliced
1 cup cooked boneless chicken, skin removed, meat cubed

C ombine chicken stock, coconut, and diet margarine in saucepan and bring to boil. Add rice, cover, and reduce heat to simmer 15 minutes. Stir in beans, onion, and chicken, and cook another 5 minutes or until liquid is absorbed.

---

### Nutritional Data

| PER SERVING | | EXCHANGES | |
|---|---|---|---|
| Calories: | 365 | Milk: | 0.0 |
| Fat (gm): | 8.1 | Vegetable: | 0.0 |
| Sat. fat (gm): | 4 | Fruit: | 0.2 |
| Cholesterol (mg): | 32.9 | Bread: | 2.3 |
| Sodium (mg): | 407 | Meat: | 1.5 |
| % Calories from fat: | 20 | Fat: | 1.0 |

# Greek Chicken and Chickpeas

**Serves 4**

4 boneless chicken breast halves, skin removed
1½ tablespoons diet margarine, melted
½ teaspoon lemon peel
¼ teaspoon ginger
¼ teaspoon cinnamon
   Dash ground black pepper
⅛ teaspoon red pepper flakes, crushed
1 15-oz. can chickpeas (garbanzo beans),
   drained and rinsed
½ cup kalamata, *or* ripe (black) olives, pitted and
   halved
¼ cup green onion, sliced
2 tablespoons olive oil

**P**reheat oven to 350 degrees. Combine melted diet margarine, lemon peel, ginger, cinnamon and pepper. Brush mixture over chicken breasts. Bake breasts uncovered 45 minutes.

Combine remaining ingredients, spoon over chicken, cover, and bake another 15 minutes.

### Nutritional Data

| PER SERVING | | EXCHANGES | |
|---|---|---|---|
| Calories: | 397 | Milk: | 0.0 |
| Fat (gm): | 13 | Vegetable: | 0.6 |
| Sat. fat (gm): | 2.1 | Fruit: | 0.0 |
| Cholesterol (mg): | 31.2 | Bread: | 2.4 |
| Sodium (mg): | 278 | Meat: | 2.0 |
| % Calories from fat: | 30 | Fat: | 2.8 |

# FARMER'S CHICKEN AND GRAVY DINNER

*Serves 6*

2 lb. whole broiler-fryer chicken, skin removed
2 tablespoons diet margarine, melted, divided
½ teaspoon salt
¼ teaspoon ground allspice
¼ cup water
**Gravy** (see recipe below)

**F**old wings to back of chicken and tie legs to tail. Combine 1 tablespoon diet margarine, salt, and allspice and brush over chicken. Add remaining diet margarine to Dutch oven, and brown chicken over medium heat 2 minutes on all sides.

Add water, cover, and cook over low heat 30-40 minutes, breast side up, until cooked through. Remove and place on serving plate, reserving pan drippings. Allow to rest 15 minutes before carving. Serve with Gravy (see recipe below).

*Gravy*

½ cup skim milk, divided
¼ cup flour
½ teaspoon salt
⅛ teaspoon ground allspice
½ cup fresh mushrooms, chopped
1 teaspoon currant jelly

Skim off fat from pan drippings. Add milk to drippings to equal 1½ cups, and pour into Dutch oven. In separate jar, combine remaining ½ cup milk, flour, salt, and allspice; cover tightly and shake well.

In Dutch oven over low heat, gradually stir milk and flour mixture into drippings mixture. Stir in mushrooms and jelly and heat to boiling, stirring constantly. Continue to boil 1 minute. Serve with Farmer's Chicken.

### Nutritional Data

| PER SERVING | | EXCHANGES | |
|---|---|---|---|
| Calories: | 256 | Milk: | 0.1 |
| Fat (gm): | 6.1 | Vegetable: | 0.1 |
| Sat. fat (gm): | 1 | Fruit: | 0.0 |
| Cholesterol (mg): | 100 | Bread: | 0.2 |
| Sodium (mg): | 521 | Meat: | 4.2 |
| % Calories from fat: | 21 | Fat: | 0.8 |

# HOT PEPPER CHICKEN

### Serves 4

½ tablespoon canola oil
½ tablespoon warm water
2 teaspoons dried marjoram
1½ teaspoons red pepper flakes
2 teaspoons diet margarine, melted
½ teaspoon salt
4 boneless chicken breast halves, skin removed

**M**ix all ingredients except chicken. Brush mixture onto both sides of chicken. Grill or broil 5-6 minutes per side, basting often, until cooked through.

### Nutritional Data

| PER SERVING | | EXCHANGES | |
|---|---|---|---|
| Calories: | 101 | Milk: | 0.0 |
| Fat (gm): | 5.3 | Vegetable: | 0.0 |
| Sat. fat (gm): | 0.9 | Fruit: | 0.0 |
| Cholesterol (mg): | 34.2 | Bread: | 0.0 |
| Sodium (mg): | 322 | Meat: | 1.5 |
| % Calories from fat: | 30 | Fat: | 1.0 |

# RED AND YELLOW CHICKEN BAKE

*Serves 4*

 1 tablespoon yellow cornmeal
1/8 teaspoon salt
1/2 teaspoon chili powder
1/4 teaspoon dried oregano
 4 boneless chicken breast halves, skin removed
 1 tablespoon diet margarine, melted
 1 tablespoon canola oil
 2 tablespoons warm water
 **Salsa** (see recipe below)

**P**reheat oven to 375 degrees. Mix together cornmeal, salt, chili powder, and oregano. Coat chicken breasts with cornmeal mixture.

Mix diet margarine, oil, and warm water and pour into baking pan. Place chicken in pan, cover, and bake 1 hour, turning once. Serve with Salsa.

*Salsa*

 1 medium tomato, chopped
 1 onion, chopped
 1 clove garlic, crushed
 1 4-oz. can jalapeño peppers, chopped
 2 teaspoons fresh cilantro, minced
 2 teaspoons lemon juice
1/4 teaspoon dried oregano

Mix all ingredients, chill, and serve with Red and Yellow Chicken.

---

### Nutritional Data

| PER SERVING | | EXCHANGES | |
|---|---|---|---|
| Calories: | 187 | Milk: | 0.0 |
| Fat (gm): | 12.5 | Vegetable: | 0.8 |
| Sat. fat (gm): | 1 | Fruit: | 0.0 |
| Cholesterol (mg): | 34.2 | Bread: | 0.2 |
| Sodium (mg): | 576 | Meat: | 1.5 |
| % Calories from fat: | 30 | Fat: | 2.0 |

# CORNUCOPIA BRAISED CHICKEN

*Serves 6*

4 boneless chicken breast halves, skin removed
3 tablespoons diet margarine, divided
½ medium onion, finely chopped
1 bay leaf
1 tablespoon curry powder
1 teaspoon salt
¼ teaspoon red pepper flakes, crushed
1½ cups hot water
1 cup dried apples
½ cup dried apricots, chopped
½ cup raisins
Sweetener equivalent to 2 tablespoons sugar
2 teaspoons instant chicken bouillon granules
2 teaspoons lemon juice
1 banana, sliced
¼ cup unsalted peanuts, chopped
2 cups cooked rice

**H**eat 2 tablespoons diet margarine in large skillet, and brown chicken over medium heat 5 minutes per side. Remove chicken with slotted spoon and set aside.

Add onion, bay leaf, curry powder, salt, and red pepper flakes to skillet and cook 4-5 minutes until onion is tender. Remove skillet from heat. Add hot water, apples, apricots, raisins, sweetener, bouillon granules, and lemon juice to skillet; mix well and return to heat. Add chicken, bring to boil, reduce heat, and simmer, covered, 30-35 minutes.

In separate skillet, melt remaining diet margarine, and heat sliced bananas over low heat. Serve chicken with heated bananas, peanuts, and hot cooked rice.

## Nutritional Data

| PER SERVING | | EXCHANGES | |
|---|---|---|---|
| Calories: | 398 | Milk: | 0.0 |
| Fat (gm): | 10.2 | Vegetable: | 0.0 |
| Sat. fat (gm): | 1.7 | Fruit: | 3.3 |
| Cholesterol (mg): | 22.9 | Bread: | 0.9 |
| Sodium (mg): | 211 | Meat: | 1.2 |
| % Calories from fat: | 22 | Fat: | 1.6 |

# 10.
# THE MAIL-ORDER CHICKEN
### Chicken & Related Culinary Supplies by Mail

**W**hy would anyone want to order a chicken by mail when they could buy one at the supermarket? If you've ever experienced the quality of a farm-raised, mail-order chicken you'll recognize the difference immediately.

For one, the birds are chemically free, and for another, they're fresh: it takes them only two days to arrive at your door. The taste difference is almost *astonishing*. Remember to request a chicken that has been properly air-chill-dressed—instantly recognizable by its bright yellow skin.

The different types of chicken indicated below are named according to their age and weight. **Broiler/fryers** are 8 to 9 weeks old, **roasters** are 12 to 14 weeks old, **poussins** are very young chickens scientifically bred for tender meat, and the sexless **capon** has been neutered to provide more tender flesh than roasters. All varieties are available smoked as well as raw or cooked.

Camden Estates
100 E. Saratoga, P.O. Box 800
Marshall, MN 56258
**(800) 282-2244**

The specialty of the house here is heat-and-serve chicken breast selections. Particularly outstanding is the chicken breast entree served with tart apple, almond, and raisin bread stuffing.

Cavanaugh Lakeview Farms
P.O. Box 580
Chelsea, MI 48118
**(800) 243-4438**

Think of this as the butcher shop in your mailbox. Although they carry many different types of game birds, chickens (including capon and poussin) are a specialty.

Craig's Original Barbecue Sauce
Cache River Enterprises
P.O. Box 272
Brinkley, AR 72021
**(501) 734-2633**

One of the grand old barbecue sauces of the South, this table sauce is for eating but not basting. The secret ingredients are the apples and oranges used instead of sugar to "soften" the taste. It's thick and rich, with pleasing hickory flavor that will make you whistle "Dixie." Available in mild, medium, or hot.

D'Artagnan
399-419 Paul Avenue
Jersey City, NJ 07306
**(201) 792-0748**
**(800) DARTAGN**

Although they are more well-known for their duck, D'Artagnan also sells free-range chickens and smoked game by mail. They are well-known in gourmet restaurant circles.

Grill Lovers Catalog
by Char Broil
P.O. Box 1300
Columbus, GA 31902-1300
**(800) 241-8981**

This is a comprehensive resource for all the grilling gadgets that help make cooking or barbecuing chicken a breeze. The Grill Lovers Catalog offers vertical roasters so the fat drips away during cooking, stir-fry baskets specially made for outdoor grills, and a full line of rotisserie accessories, including a tumble basket that's perfect for chicken. A good source for clean-up supplies and brushes!

# 11.
# THE LITERARY CHICKEN

♦ **Books**

*Chicken Cookbook*
by the Editors of Classic Pillsbury Cookbooks

*Cooking Light: Poultry*
by the Editors of Warner Books

*Healthy Chicken*
by Barbara Chernetz

*Six Ingredients or Less Chicken Cookbook*
by Carlean Johnson

## ◆ *Video*

*"Chicken and Poultry"*
Cooking at the Academy Videos
California Culinary Academy
San Francisco School of Cooking
**(800) 229-2433 ext. 232**

## ◆ *Pamphlets*

3 free chicken brochures from the National Broiler Council:

*Chicken: Its Nutritive Value*

*Chicken: How To Cut and Bone It*

*Chicken: Food For Fitness*
c/o Communications Division
P.O. Box 5806
2817 Millwood Avenue
Columbia, SC 29250
**(803) 254-8158**

*Preventing Foodborne Illness: A Guide to Safe Food Handling*
U.S. Department of Agriculture
Home and Garden Bulletin Number 247
Food Safety Information Division
14th and Independence Avenue S.W., Room 8-E
Washington, DC 20250
**(202) 720-2109**

## ◆ *Hotline*

USDA Meat and Poultry Hotline:
**(800) 535-4555**

# INDEX